art as prayer

Visual Communion with God

---

by Eric Nykamp

For the Creative Community
at Madison Square Church

table of contents

Part Three – The Prayer of the Hand

Part Four – The Prayer of the Moment

—

a word of thanks

I am hoping some day to visit the North West Coast of North America, because I am captivated by the culture and artwork of the Native Americans and First Peoples indigenous to that area. In particular, I want to see the varieties of totem poles, which are carved in that region.

I often think of totem poles when I think of the people in my life who have impacted me. I think of the many people upon whose shoulders I stand – the many people who have gone before me, who have cleared the path I am walking on. I am hoping in turn to clear the path a bit for those who come after me as well.

So to begin this book, I want to thank the many people who have influenced me over the years, whose impact on my life is reflected in the pages you hold in your hand.

Thank you to:

- My parents, who bought me the "make it" box when I was little, and kept it stocked with art supplies. Thank you for encouraging my artistic gifts.
- My parents, who continually built me up and

—

gave me a safe home when childhood bullies hurt me when my artistic tendencies made me "different" from how country boys were "supposed to be." Thank you for encouraging me to be who God made me to be, in spite of what our local culture taught.

- My dad, who made me easels, built frames for my paintings, and helped me create the other supplies I needed over the years to make increasingly professional art.
- Thank you to my many art teachers over the years, especially Ms. Pories, who not only encouraged me to express my heart to God through art, but also encouraged me to express my heart to her after school many times when I felt lost.
- Thank you to my art professors at Calvin College, especially Professor Overvoorde, who challenged me to think about how to use art to express ideas of faith in numerous ways. Thank you also for encouraging and mentoring me when I was in a dark place, and seeing me as a worthwhile person to invest in when my art was full of anger and frustration at my life and the world.
- Thank you to my wife, Yee Lam, who has loved me because and in spite of my artistic temperament through the years.
- Thank you, Yee Lam, for encouraging me when I felt I needed to paint and you needed me to do other things that needed to be attended to. Thank you for helping me find balance while encouraging me to see that there does not have to be a choice between making art and

—

taking care of the routine business of life.
- Thank you too, Yee Lam, for nurturing and walking with me through these past few years when I didn't think I could ever paint again after my attack. Thank you for loving me when I didn't feel very loveable.
- Thank you to Yee Lam's dad, my father in law, who asked me the question "How can I look at and understand art?", which is the basis of this book.
- Thank you to the artists at Madison Square Church who have been part of the Creative Community group there. Thank you for being a body of Christians who actively wrestle with issues of faith and creativity. Thank you for the chance to laugh together, and for these long friendships over the years.
- Thank you to Dorwin, who encouraged me to take the lessons I wrote for Creative Community and try to publish them. You kicked my butt in the best sense possible ... and challenged me to walk in faith to use words to help others understand non-verbal expression. I never would have thought of this on my own. I sincerely believe that God used you to have this impact on my life.
- Thank you to the members of GR CIVA (Grand Rapids Christians in the Visual Arts) for all the meetings and friendships – all those times where each month we spent exploring our twin loves for art and God.
- Thank you to Madison Square Church and especially the Antioch group there for challenging me to press on using the visual in

—

worship, despite the roughness of the road.

- Thank you to Audrey, for mentoring me, loving me, and encouraging me to use my gifts ... and for loving me in spite of my old habit of sending angry emails. Thank you for forgiving me and caring for me in spite of my ugly side.
- Thank you to all those members of the church staff who walked with me, prayed with me, and heard my sorrows and fears that I poured out to you over the years. You have loved me when I was in the valley, and you held me up when I didn't have the strength.
- Thank you to my care group, who loves me no matter what. I love all of you too. We belong to each other.
- Thank you to Sharon, who not only is my visual prayer partner (we speak that same visual language), but also bought me a little professional watercolor set when I had not painted for a year, encouraging me to paint again. You believed in me when I could not believe. Thank you for loving me with this thoughtful gift. I now am learning to paint with tears and paint. Thank you for caring for my heart and seeing what I could be again.
- Thank you to Julie, whose artwork is a luminous, calligraphic visual prayer. You always inspire me. Thank you for having breakfast with me, sharing your own story so I did not feel alone. Thank you for looking at my watercolor sketches and telling me that this was good art, even though it was so different from my last decade of work. Thank you for telling me that they were beautiful.

—

- Thank you to Chris for letting me play with the letterpress to get my creative juices going again. Thank you for opening my eyes to the expressive qualities of type.
- Thank you to all my children who often sit and draw with me, or on your own in the art studio, which you now inhabit more than me. May God continue to smile on you as you continue to discover all those wonderful qualities that God has planted in you. I love you all (and yes, I know I tell you that every day).

To all my friends and traveling companions,

Thank you.
Eric Nykamp
November 15, 2011

—

My heart says of you "Seek his face!"
Your face, Lord, I will seek."
It's just really hard sometimes ...

introduction

Let the message of Christ
dwell among you richly as you
teach and admonish one
another with all wisdom
through psalms, hymns and
songs from the Spirit,
singing to God with
gratitude in your hearts.

Colossians 3:16

I am an artist and a Christian · who has been
deeply hurt by the church. I know there is
nothing particularly unique about being hurt by
the church. I think most people who go to church
have been hurt at one time or another by
someone else in the congregation. We all hurt
each other sometimes (myself included) and need
to continually practice how to both apologize and
forgive. My particular hurt may be a little

—

unusual, however. I wrestle with using my artistic gifts, my *visual* artistic gifts, in the church and in worship.

I sometimes get very angry about this. I struggle with feelings of resentment, of frustration, of being misunderstood or overlooked. It is quite easy for me to complain about how "those church people don't get me". But I don't want to go there. It is too easy. I have had so many of those conversations with people over the years... and it goes nowhere. It just makes me angry and bitter, and I want to learn a better way.

I am not always an easy person to love. I have a lot of rough edges, bad habits, and imperfections I would not want to put down on paper because looking at them would cause me to feel such shame. My church loves me in spite of my shadow side. They love me, and they also don't always understand me.

I know God understands me, and it took me many years to accept that my times of visual communion with God as an artist were valuable to God, a way for God to surround me with His presence while I spoke to him with the language of paint and pen. It is because I have come to accept that God created me to be with Him this way, as a visual artist, that I want to come back and try to share what this is like with my fellow church friends who may understand words much better than pictures. For this reason, I am writing these letters, so that you may understand this kind of aesthetic prayer language.

So I want people, especially church people, to ask me questions about my work. I am quite familiar with the kinds of questions people ask. Some people are curious about how I craft my paintings, some people are interested in asking me about the thoughts that go into my work, some people want to get a sense for what I believe my work could mean. These are all good questions. I want my work to engage people's minds the way creating art engages my own imagination.

However, some questions cause me to pause. I recall one conversation I had with a dear friend who, after listening to me talk about my work, asked me if I could teach him how to look at paintings so that he too could feel that he understood them. He asked me to teach him how to see a painting for what it means. I remember feeling a sense of sadness take over my mind, realizing that something that brought me such joy and a sense of the presence of a creative God was completely missing from my friend's experience. He saw himself as without the ability to perceive what for me was a basic part of life – too see God in art. The realization that he was not unlike many other people that I knew caused powerful emotions to well up within me.

—

The writing that follows has taken me many months of pouring over my answer to the question "How can I look at, and understand, art?" I have started my answer to this question several times, becoming frustrated often. There is no simple answer, no formulaic process to apply. How do I allow someone to look through my eyes? Yet, this question is such a common one that I feel the need to at least attempt an answer.

What I came up with (and subsequently have written down here) is taken mainly from a talk that I developed entitled "Art as Prayer" which I have spent the last year presenting both to gatherings of creative artists and to church congregations alike. This material has been gathered from both my own experiences as well as my conversations with many creative Christians that I am fortunate to call my friends – friends that have opened up their lives to me to share their experiences as children of God made in the image of the Great Creator.

While most of what I am going to talk about will be peppered with my experiences as a visual artist, these general ideas apply to other fields of creativity as well – feels as diverse as dance, writing, music composition, sermon writing, and the various visual art forms.

—

It is my hope that you will find your mind opened
as we share this creative journey together.

—

part one – foundational ideas

HEAR MY PRAYER, O GOD

on words

There are different kinds of gifts, but the same Spirit distributes them. There are different kinds of service, but the same Lord. There are different kinds of working, but in all of them and in everyone it is the same God at work.

I Corinthians 12: 4-6

It was an unusually rainy day when I was sitting with my father-in-law in his apartment. His flat on the sixth floor of a high-rise in Hong Kong overlooking a park where on clear days you can see people gather doing tai chi down below. But this was a rainy day, and no one was outside except to scurry, umbrellas in hand, to the nearby subway station inside the neighboring mall. As the rain gently blew into fine streaks across the window, our conversation wandered from the weather eventually to talking about art. Now

—

there is one thing you must know about my father-in-law. He is a world-traveled theologian, and a creative one at that. This is evident in the many books that he has written over his lengthy career. We often have very provocative discussions when we have stretches of time to talk together. I often find that he has thought long about many things, understanding the richness of ideas and topics in ways that help my own ideas to blossom. So it was a surprise when he asked me "Can you teach me how to look at and understand art?" This question came as a surprise to me how someone with such a deep understanding of many things had no idea how to look at a painting, and come away with some new insights or understanding.

At first, I did not know what to say. As an artist, looking at art and creating it is second nature to me. It is like reading a novel or going to a concert – art moves me emotionally as well as intellectually at times. But his question opened my eyes to the fact that this is not necessarily the case for everyone. For many people, the world of visual art is populated by people whose strange and foreign customs render their expressions inscrutable and mysterious. Rather than making the invisible visible, visual artists often just seem to be contributing to the fog clouding the camera lens of understanding for many people who want to understand visual art.

—

I don't recall how I responded to his question. However, it was one of those rare questions in life that I pondered for some time to come. I came to see that maybe I needed to at least try to clear the fog for my father-in-law, and anyone else who wants to see art enlighten their own imagination.

Maybe you are one of those people. If so, I am writing to you, and am glad that you invested time in reading these pages to try to understand what for me is one of the true joys of life. So let's begin this journey together.

As an artist, I typically find that the way I am best able to express myself is to create a painting – an image without words. I now find myself sitting before a computer attempting to express myself with words – a means of communication that at times feels awkward as I find myself wanting to "show you" what I mean when I need to be writing it out. This tension causes me to chuckle. For you, I will resort to words to attempt to explain to you how to look at and understand art.

Before I begin, I need to tell you that I struggled a long time with feeling sad that you were having difficulty understanding art. For me, creating and looking at art is such a wonderful thing. I feel so connected to God while I am making a painting, and when looking at work in a gallery, I feel in a way like I am surrounded by the spirits of the artists whose work surrounds me – a sense that I

—

am understood for who I was created to be – an artist. I wish that you could share this sense with me, and I will try to help you as best I can so that you can experience this for yourself, even if only to a small degree at first. Thank you for wanting to understand this part of me, which is so close to my heart.

In a way, this is like walking with a person who has just come to know God. Such a person is full of hope and desire, yet full of questions as well. They understand only grace, but isn't this the most important thing? I hope that you too come away with a sense of the presence of God through the journey that I am about to walk with you. At times I think you may find my way silly or strange, but I ask you to continue persevering. I will be walking with you, and if I sense you finding me odd, it may break my heart. I don't open up like this too often.

Many people want to experience the presence of God, and the church has rightly been the vehicle through which people have often come to experience Him. Yet, it is my conviction that the church has only just begun to discover how to convey the transforming power of God to those we are called to serve. Though God has given His children five senses through which to discover and understand His world, the church (most prominently the Protestant church) has focused primarily on the sense of hearing as the route by which to communicate about God. Even the

—

sense of hearing has been subdivided – with prominence given to listening to speech as the primary vehicle by which people come to know God. Now, I do not disagree that verbal communication is powerful and effective. God primarily passed on to us information about Himself through the written words of the Bible. But an exclusive or near exclusive focus on the spoken, preached, and sung words of scripture seems at times to overlook other powerful means of communicating the nature and essence of these ideas.

I heard the theologian William Dyrness speak recently about this very thing. He stated that only 40% of people (in the cultures he has studied) are verbal learners. He speculated that this is likely true of all cultures the world over, and that this fact has ramifications for the church who has traditionally relied heavily on transmitting the ideas of the gospel through verbal means. This is a great departure from the challenge St. Francis of Assissi spoke of when he instructed his follower to "preach the Gospel at all times and when necessary use words." How many other methods of preaching the gospel have we overlooked by solely relying on communicating our message using verbal means?

This has been born out in my experiences as an artist. Many people seem to be intrigued by the visual means by which I experience God, but

—

seem to find themselves visually illiterate. Is it possible that churches are filled with the 40% of people who are primarily verbally oriented, and that many of the visual people like myself remain un-reached outside the doors?

Being a Protestant believer, I look back at the history of my branch of Christianity and feel a sense of sadness. In reaction to the abuses of the church at the time, the Protestant movement declared that visual art, dancing, and in some cases even musical accompaniment to singing had no place in the life of the church, thereby relegating non-verbal expressions in worship as irrelevant and dangerous... for the next 400 years. It was at this point in the history of Western Civilization that the creative community began its transition from religious employment to secular society, a movement that in many ways we are seeing the fruit of today – where the creative products of our society often seem fueled by anti-Christian sentiments and no longer reflect the values or even wrestle with the ideas of communities of faith.

My friend, as I write this letter to you, I would hope that you could in part understand my sadness at seeing the church reject the gifts of some of God's creative children. I often wonder what would have happened in the Protestant church if creative artists were involved in the decisions that shaped the Reformation. If you are to understand me, first you need to understand

—

my grief over the historical loss of much of the church's imagination. God, forgive us.

God help heal us, and bring us together again. Help us to understand each other, love each other, and encourage each other.

Amen.

Take this, God. Take it from me, please

intimacy with God

*Love the Lord your God
with all your heart and with
all your soul and with all your
mind and with all your
strength.*

Mark 12:30

Today I was remembering the time I decided I no
longer wanted to go to church. I was seventeen
years old, and had been going to church all my
life. I was growing close to God, especially close
in the last two years of High School, but was
feeling a growing disconnect to how I related to
God and the ways that I was taught in my church.
Church was a place filled with words about God.
Words spoken, often angrily it seemed, from the
pulpit. Words often warning about how the
corrupt culture was seducing us, words
implicating youth and youth culture especially as
the prime culprits of societal decay. Words were
sung by the congregation, but as I would turn to

look at the faces of those singing the words, there were no smiles or even bodily indicators of joy. Church was an perplexingly somber affair.

Intimacy with God was often encouraged to take place through verbal routes. "Good Christians" sought this intimacy through the following formula:

1. Reading the words of the Bible at home.
2. Listening to the words of Christian songs on the radio.
3. Reading words written by Christian authors (nearly exclusively non-fiction).
4. Speaking words to God through verbal prayers.
5. Listening to the words of scripture from the pulpit.
6. Hearing the interpretation of these words of scripture through the words of the pastor's sermon.
7. Reciting the scripted words of "responsive readings" aloud as a congregation. (These were never spontaneous, responsive expressions of the congregation members speaking for themselves)
8. Singing words of hymns in church.

It was taught that by doing these things, that intimacy with God would be achieved. But somehow, it seemed to fall short for me. I needed to use my body. In church the only times that I heard about how to use my body to please God were times in which we were instructed on what to *abstain from doing* with our bodies. There was little teaching on the positive aspects of what we could do with our physical bodies, no teaching on how to employ the senses to experience God, and seldom was a sense of awe or wonder invoked during a worship service. The idea of artistically crafting a worship experience on Sundays was unheard of. While services had logical and theological unity, the routine of worship all but ignored any concerns for aesthetics or personal expression. The longer I attended there, the more I began to feel emotionally suffocated in church.

Once out of my pew, I experienced a different God - a God who loved to explore the world with me, a God of potential, a God who cried when we His children suffered. I began to go on mission trips to work with people living in poverty as a teenager. I could sense God in the streets of the inner city. I had an awareness of God when I heard someone speak some words I believed God wanted me to pay particular attention to. I felt God when I used my body to serve Him. I began to wonder if I could use my artistic gifts to serve God as well. I wondered what would happen if I served God the way I was feeling moved to do so.

While I was blessed to be exposed to the fundamental ideas of Christianity through the words of the church, these words were not

—

enough for me to feel close to God. I needed more, something relational, something "real". I wanted to do more than know about God, I wanted to know God. The singer Charlie Peacock had written a song around that time that included the following lines:

> *I want to know you,*
> *Not just about you.*
> *Teach me secrets such as these.*

This song in many ways became my personal prayer to God that I sang over and over through the coming years, a song whose simplicity and earnestness called to my heart. It was not where I was at that time, but it was where I wanted to go.

I liken my relationship with God at that point in time to a marriage where the partners never touched each other. I was spending a lot of time reading about how to have a good relationship, and even at times spoke about this relationship · but I didn't spend time listening. I did listen to love songs that put me in a relationally minded mood, but what did I do with these feelings? My early relationship to Christ was a relationship played out in my head alone. In many ways, until I engaged my body with my mind, the marriage was never consummated.

—

Maybe you feel this way as well. Has the passion gone out of your relationship to God? Are you like me, a person who early on felt a burning for God, yet once past the first few years of the relationship no longer had fuel to stoke the fire? Are you like the couple I saw in a restaurant once, both reading the newspaper while having dinner – never speaking a word to each other except to conclude by asking "Are you done?" Do you want to hold hands with God, but have busied yourself only by passing notes?

The solution may be in your hands – literally. We are instructed in scripture to love God with our mind and our strength. We have lots of examples on how to love God with our minds, but what about the rest of the equation? Let us explore this more together through the next few pages.

As you read, imagine God with you, reading along side you. God is, in fact, with you as you read, though I don't think we often think of this. Try to think about what it is that God wants you to perceive as you read these words. Ask God to guide your heart and your imagination to be open to whatever it is that you are to think about. Maybe in this way, with God's help, you may come to understand how to look at a piece of art, and have some understanding of what it could mean. It is my prayer, my hope, that God will give you this blessing with time.

—

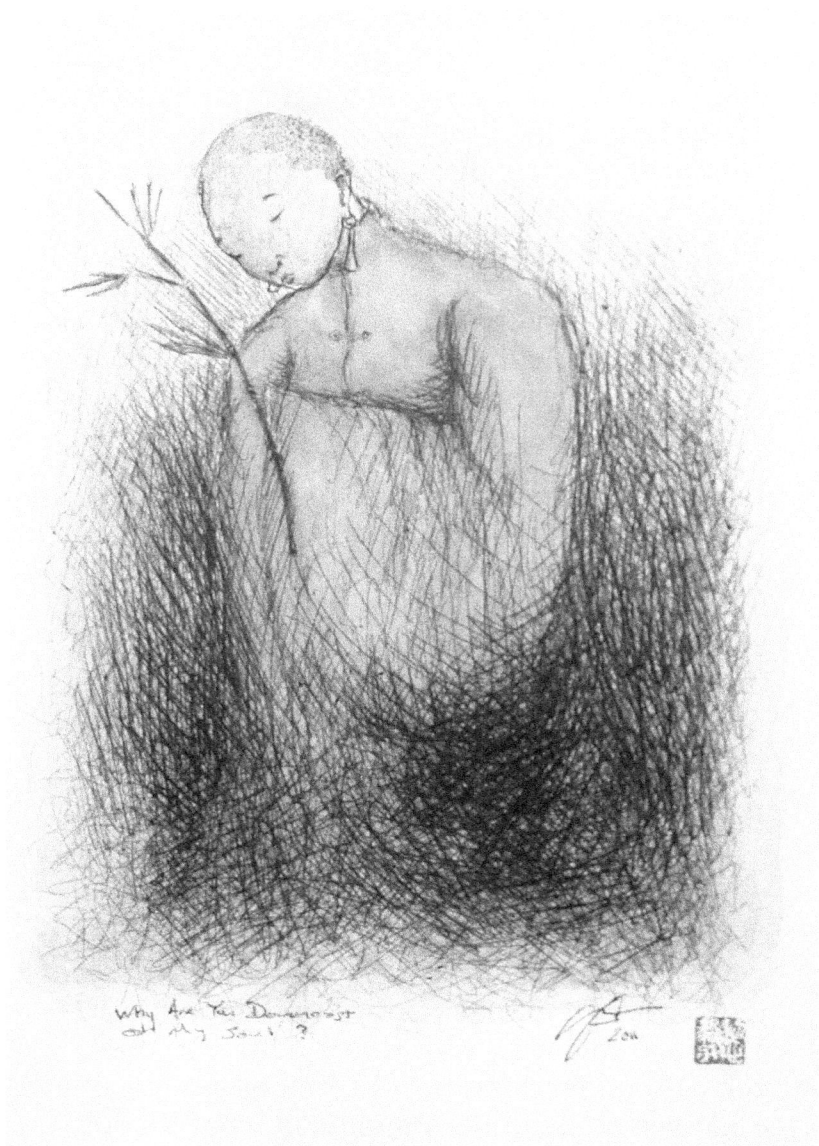

Why Are You Demanding
on My Soul?

2011

pray without speaking

Be still, and know that I am God.

Psalm 46:10a

I want to tell you about a seminar that I went to the other day. I friend handed me a brochure on a short talk on something called "Contemplative Prayer". The meeting was over a lunch hour, and I decided to attend. I thought that there would be very few people there. To my surprise, the room was full. The speaker was an interesting man. Tall, wearing a suit coat with no tie, his grey hair slightly tossed about as his little round glasses kept sliding down his nose. But as he quietly spoke to the packed room, what he was talking about captured my imagination. He was speaking about "centering" prayer.

As an art student, I recall first hearing the word "centering" in the context of throwing clay on a potter's wheel. "Centering" the clay, means to gently but firmly shape a spinning ball of clay from an off-balance, slippery lump into a perfectly

—

centered form in the middle of the wheel. Too much pressure and the clay would go shooting off the edge of the wheel – torn from its base. Two little force, and my arm would be repeatedly struck by the blunt bulges of the lump, making my hand bounce and sputter across its surface. But once centered, a potter can begin to form the clay into a vessel. This is the starting point from which the artist can begin to work. Centering is preparation, and even though it requires the most physical strength, centering alone will still only leave you with an unformed lump of clay – but clay that is ready for change.

As the presenter spoke, he talked about how he "centers" himself, first reading the words of scripture like a love letter written from God to him, then selecting a word or phrase that he finds meaningful, using this as the phrase with which he prays[1]. Closing his eyes, and finding a comfortable position, he led us in trying this ourselves, meditating and reflecting on a word or a few words from scripture, seeing what prayerful imaginings came from just sitting still and thinking about these words.

In the silence, I felt God, surrounding me.

I left the room feeling energized, like I had discovered some well-kept secret and was excited

---

[1] This ancient form of prayer is known as Lectio Divina.

with this new discovery. But trying this at home was another thing. Small children running about, shrieking intermittently with delight, the jingle of the telephone, the hum of the dryer, and the sounds of my wife moving about the house all distracted me. What seemed so simple and easy presented itself as a challenge. When I figured out how to keep from being distracted by me ears, my mind began to fill with thoughts, ideas, worries, and pictures. My interior world is as busy as the exterior world I live in. I came to find that the clutter I find about me as well as within me is highly stimulating, not to mention utterly distracting. The world of things and thoughts was completely getting in the way of doing something as simple as taking some time to think about the God who is around me all the time, every day.

Have you ever felt this kind of distraction when you pray? It happens to me all the time. The times I try to focus silently on God become times interrupted by mental chatter... and it is my own fault. My heart seems to sense the need for this kind of "being with" God, yet I leave frustrated time and time again when I try to be still in the presence of God.

I crave special, intimate time alone with God. Yet, it seems so foreign to me. I want a relationship with God that is like a close friendship, the kind of closeness that I saw while standing in a public square in Chu Chao in Southern China. While standing in the darkness of early evening, silk lanterns from Chinese New Year like luminous red jellyfish danced from strings hanging above our heads while my wife, father-in-law and I watched the crowds in a square by a fountain. Teenagers were milling about, and chains of girls holding hands together would emerge periodically from the throngs. My father-in-law remarked that it was good that girls still felt comfortable holding hands in public, as where he lived in Hong Kong, this seemed to be a dying tradition. These girls were friends who felt close enough that they could touch each other without embarrassment. They had a kind of love for each other that can only be born out of deep, lifelong friendship. They belonged to each other, as their linked hands showed so vividly as they walked past in their cheerful, brightly colored New Year's jackets.

God, I want to know you like that – like lifelong friends walking together. We already walk together, but I still want to feel you near me.

My friend, I want you to know God like this as well. What I want to tell you about next is another way to find God in the stillness that the gray-haired speaker had yet to explore. To me, this seems like my powerful secret that I just can't wait to share, if you can keep from being distracted long enough to hear what it is.

—

—

seeing God

The Word became flesh and made his dwelling among us. We have seen his glory, the glory of the one and only [Son], who came from the Father, full of grace and truth.

John 1:14

I have been doing a lot of reading lately about people who describe moments when they felt close to God. I am not talking about stories were people describe angel sightings or dramatic displays of the power of God (though I believe in both these things, this is not the focus of what I want to write to you about). What impressed me is that these stories are written by seemingly regular people, doing common things, in common places. There is nothing noteworthy of spectacular about what they were doing when they felt that they encountered God. But

—

something happened that transformed their ordinary experience into something extraordinary. What these stories all have in common is that these experiences have a dramatic, visual element to them. In other words, these people have unique experiences in which they each *see* God.

- A writer shares about walking in a desert near her home when she sees a bird making a home in a cactus. This becomes a visual reminder of how God protects her even among hardships in her own life.

- A poet sees his own struggle with a crippling physical disability in a new light when his friends give birth to their first child who comes to develop the same condition that he has. Being close friends with the child's parents, he has intimate access to perceiving how they love their newborn son unconditionally just as he is. In watching this family, he gets a fresh sense of how God cares for him, loving him as he is, and not as someone whose identity is tied to being "broken and pitied."

- I met an artist[2] who takes pieces of junk and welds them into sculptural crosses,

---

[2] This artist is James Quinten Young

—

describing the process as a reminder of what it means to be rescued and redeemed.

These experiences all allow us to see God literally, or through the mental images these stories create in our imaginations. It is the power of narrative, the power of sight.

Many people speak of times that they have felt close to God using descriptive language, telling stories of moments when God gave them an image, revealed Himself through nature or through dreams. What makes these visual images so powerful?

This is not a phenomenon that is isolated to these contemporary times when people look for proof of the existence of God. Reading through scripture, many of the Old and New Testament writers spent long passages *describing* images, dreams, and events that they witnessed. Why would God find it important to spend so many words describing these things if the visual (or for that matter the non-verbal) aspects of Christianity were not implicitly necessary for the understanding of the gospel message? What I am coming more and more to believe is that the Biblical God is a visual God. Let me explain.

—

From all points in scripture, the Bible is filled with descriptions of the visual and non-verbal aspects of faith – elements that are necessary for a balanced understanding of the verbal and cerebral aspects of faith. The Bible begins with a poetic passage describing the creation of the world followed by a story that recounts in more detail the drama of the last moments in that narrative. Later on, there are detailed descriptions of how God wanted the tabernacle to be constructed – details as specific as the names of the people he wanted in charge of creating the artwork and the exact composition of the incense used in worship. God did not leave these things up to interpretation, He took a direct hand in how he wanted things designed so that the worship space would thereby shape His worship. The prophets too spend page after page verbally painting dream imagery while the history books describe the monuments, sacrifices, dances, and music of the day.

But in the New Testament, the non-verbal aspects of Christianity become even stronger. God becomes a person that we can see, allowing us as people to touch Him, hear Him, and eat with Him. He told stories, taking ordinary things and using them to illustrate spiritual ideas – transforming the vision of all who heard so that they would be reminded of these tales when they saw these objects again in their daily lives. To make this even more obvious, the ultimate proof of the Gospel was visual – the bodily resurrection of

—

Jesus from the dead. That is why I believe that the Biblical God is a visual God.

I find this idea liberating as an artist because so often I am told (implicitly or explicitly at times) that my gifts cannot be used in the church, or that they can be used but only in limited and greatly reduced degrees. For example, for years there have been powerful disagreements among church staff about hanging artwork in our narthex for art displays. For some reason, putting a nail in a wall seems to require more committees and approvals than it takes to start a fundraising campaign. When artwork is used, there is such scrutiny over making sure that the art does not offend or challenge anyone, that many artists have stopped trying to use their art in the church altogether. Many of the artists mutter to each other how the pastor's messages do not need pre-approval from anyone before they are spoken from the pulpit, but the artists must have their work combed over by a committee before it is given permission to be hung. It leaves many of the artists wondering why there is so much fuss and mistrust of the way they want to offer their service to God and the church.

Now, I may sound a bit bitter (and to be truthful, I do feel some hurt when I write about this), but I do not want you to mistake my periodic frustrations with an outright hatred of the church. I love my church deeply; in spite of the ways it frustrates and disappoints me from time to time

—

(and they love me too, even though I certainly have my moments of "unlovable-ness"!). My church is not unique in this regard. Many churches have great difficulty with figuring out how to use art forms they are not accustomed to using.   From an artist's perspective, it sometimes feels like what could have happened if J.S. Bach had been an unknown musician. Now imagine that Bach, the unknown musician, had to go to his church council to beg their permission to play a piece on the organ that he felt would glorify God. Now picture the council meeting and after a long "discussion", coming back to J.S. and telling him that he would be allowed to play, but only if he used one finger until the congregation "got used" to the idea of organ music in worship. In this imaginary scenario, it would indeed be a good step forward to allow Bach to play a tune on the organ, but it would most certainly not actualize the awesome potential Bach had as an organist and composer. Too often, this is what it feels like to be a visual artist in the church.

Now creative artists often find that they must work within their communities, meeting their aesthetic needs starting from where they are. In fact, it is an honorable thing to be so committed to your church that you want to pursue using your artwork there rather than opportunities in another more public and well-respected forum or gallery space. But it is a difficult problem to both feel the creative urge and yet restrain it at the same time. Churches and artists definitely need each

—

other, but sometimes the places from which they approach each other feel very far apart. A middle ground may be a great distance from where each imagined they would end.

I hope that as I tell you this that you can both hear my frustration, and yet know that I love the church. I am aware that you have been asking me to teach you how to understand art, and what I have been talking about in the last few paragraphs may seem a great digression from that topic. I think for you to know how to look at art, it first is necessary to understand the people who make art – people who are not much different from you. We want to pour ourselves into our work – creative work – for the glory of God. It feels good to work on something, struggle with it, and end up with a finished product, be it a story, a piece of music, a dance, or another work of art. The tension comes in the fact that when we go to offer these aesthetics gifts to God in the church, that there is at times a less-than-receptive air that surrounds both the gift and the giver. We as artists sometimes feel a great deal of tension with the church, churches that will take our tithes, but not the work of our hands. It is difficult for us to understand. And yet, for those of us who remain, we still love our faith and our brothers and sisters in Christ. We love them, standing firm in the knowledge that the visual has a role to play in the life of the church, only that culturally the church is not always in a place to perceive this. We hold on to hope that just as

—

God continues to pour gifts of visual creativity into his children that these skills are being used more and more in the church. The good news is that the cultural resistance to using the talents of visual artists in the church is eroding, even if some days it is hard to perceive!

I appreciate that you are asking questions about understanding art. It gives me hope that at least you will be able to understand me, or at least understand me a little bit more. Thank you for listening to me as I write these letters. I deeply appreciate it.

Falling

balanced meals

This is the account of Noah
and his family.
Noah was a righteous man,
blameless among the people
of his time, and he walked
faithfully with God.

Genesis 6:9

A few months ago I ended up in the emergency room, full of pain, and wondering what was wrong with my body. I had been going to the urgent care clinic a few days in a row, as I was having terrible pain that was diagnosed differently on each visit. I finally drove myself to the ER, enduring the hours of waiting until I could finally be seen. I had to lie down in some kind of a machine to take a picture of my insides. What they discovered was that I had three kidney stones that were all at different stages of working their way out of my body.

—

I was sent to a specialist to learn about why I suddenly started developing kidney stones. The recommendations that I received were mostly dietary – I needed to eat different foods and drink way more fluids... or I would risk having this pain again.

I started to examine my diet. I love salty foods, and I overate them a great deal. I needed to avoid so many savory foods, which was very troubling to me. I craved those foods. Maybe it was all in my head, but abstaining or reducing my intake of these foods seemed impossible at first. But gradually, over the last few months, I have been making changes and am on my way to developing a healthier, more balanced diet.

And in doing this, I had a thought. The dietary changes that I am making are much like the changes I hope to see the church develop some day. We need to balance our religious diets by developing sensitivities to commune with God in a variety of ways. As things are at present, it seems that the worship of God has an overly verbal approach, and that the non-verbal approaches have been neglected. But things are beginning to move the other way, slowly.

I have been writing to you about the way we church people have come to know God through verbal means. In many ways, these are the essential ways to begin knowing about God.

—

Learning through words is an important way to come to know God, but it is not the only way. I think of words as the "meat and potatoes" of the Christian diet (or "meat and rice", "rice and beans", or "fufu", depending on the culture you are coming from). If all you eat is meat and potatoes, however, you will end up in the hospital like me, in pain because of dietary imbalance. No. We have a need for other flavors, other entire food groups, and other cuisines. The balanced Christian diet must include regular times of non-verbal communion with God.

I use the word "communion" here intentionally. To "commune" with God is different than "communicating" with God. Many of us think of closeness to God as being able to communicate with Him, and I don't want to neglect the importance of communicating with God. Talking, writing, singing and reading about God are all important ways of developing a closer relationship with God. But can you see the verbal-bias in even the language the church has to describe closeness to God? We often ask people what God is "saying" to us lately, or even telling people to "listen" for God. I propose a change in language, which I hope will then shape the way we even conceptualize our relationship with God.

Instead of asking each other what God has been "saying" to us, could we not ask what God is "showing" us or "revealing" to us lately? Could

—

we shift from "listening" for God to "waiting" for or "being with" God? Could we go back to the lines of an old Christian song, and sing that *"He walks with me and He talks with me..."*, a lyric that parallels the verbal and non-verbal relationship that God had with Adam and Eve in the garden before the fall. Could we shift from communicating with God to communing with Him? Could we?

More than anything, I want to create an environment in the church that is welcoming to creative people again. That will take a lot of gradual changes, I know. Knowing that you continue to read these letters from me gives me encouragement that at least you are willing to try to know my heart and make room in your heart to understand me. It means a lot to me that you do this... more than you probably even know.

—

—

He will hide me

learning to remember

But in fact God has placed the parts in the body, every one of them, just as he wanted them to be.

1 Corinthians 12:18

When I was young, I had some trouble learning in school. I found that I had such difficulty spelling, and later, I found that I had tremendous difficulty learning foreign languages – a problem that prevented me from pursuing my childhood dream of becoming a pastor. My mother, who returned to graduate school to get a Masters in Education when I was in third grade, was taking classes on helping children to learn in unique ways. She began trying to teach me at home in the evenings using some of the ideas that she was learning about in graduate school. I feel very fortunate to have grown up in a family culture that allowed me to discover the way that I learned best, which allowed me to get passing grades in school if I applied myself and worked hard outside of class.

—

Going through High School, I remember that the art room in many ways became the sanctuary for many kids who did not do well in other academic courses... but in art they excelled and were able to show their giftedness. In college, I noticed a similar pattern. At the end of the BFA program, all of us were required to take a class for art majors called "senior seminar" in which we talked about what to do with our degree after graduation. One particular day the professor opened the class by asking how many of us had ever been told that we had a learning disability. Most of the students raised their hands. The reason that I am sharing this is not to imply that creative people all have learning disabilities. Quite the contrary. I am sharing these stories to illustrate a point – our culture values certain ways of showing intelligence more than others. But there are many ways that a person can express their intelligence... yet too often people in higher education, talk therapy, and churches tend to reinforce the cultural bias towards verbal and mathematical intelligence over other ways of expressing intelligence.

Let me explain what I am getting at here. In order to do so, I need to briefly share with you a bit about learning theory, namely, the theory of multiple intelligences. The main idea of this theory is that there are quite a number of ways that people learn, and express themselves. There is no singular method to teach something in a way that most people will learn and retain

—

information. Dr. Howard Gardner, professor of education at Harvard University, developed this theory in 1983. Up until this time, people assumed that people's ability to learn was based on an innate ability to learn, called an "intelligence quotient" or IQ. But what Dr. Gardner proposed (and since has been found to be valid by many researchers) is that there are seven different kinds of intelligence, which account for a broader range of human potential in children and adults. These seven intelligences are:

Verbal-linguistic	"word smart"
Musical-rhythmic	"music smart"
Logical-mathematical	"number and reasoning smart"
Visual-spatial	"picture smart"
Bodily-kinesthetic	"body smart"
Interpersonal	"people smart"
Intrapersonal	"self smart"

I often give talks on this theory to church groups, talking just a little about each kind of intelligence to explain the theory. I will often have group members identify each way that they feel comfortable learning by standing when I describe one of the ways in which they learn best. People are amazed to see that there is no one style of learning that most people learn best by. Most information would need to be taught in about 3-4 styles simultaneously for an entire group to learn something.

What does that tell us? I always marvel at how affirming it is to people (many of whom never knew this kind of information) to hear that they are not stupid for having difficulty learning by reading, listening to someone talk, or reasoning (the way much instruction is done in Western cultures). In fact, it seems quite scriptural to conclude that God created all of us with this internal diversity to make the world an interesting place! In 1 Corinthians 12:12, Paul explains, "Just as a body, though one, has many parts, but all its many parts form one body, so it is with Christ." He goes on to describe how we should not reject each other based on our differences, but instead see these differences as gifts which each contribute to the health of the body as a whole.

This idea is further born out in the "learning pyramid" which succinctly illustrates how much information is retained based on the way in which the information is taught. To summarize the numbers (which sometimes get cited differently) learners retain approximately:

—

5% of what they learn when they've learned from lecture.
10% of what they learn when they've learned from reading.
20% of what they learn from audio-visual.
30% of what they learn when they see a demonstration.
50% of what they learn when engaged in a group discussion.
75% of what they learn when they practice what they learned.
90% of what they learn when they teach someone else/use immediately.

What always strikes me about this is that the more senses that are involved in learning, the better the retention. For visual artists, the learning pyramid is especially affirming as it skillfully shows how the use of visual expression greatly aids people in the retention of information.

—

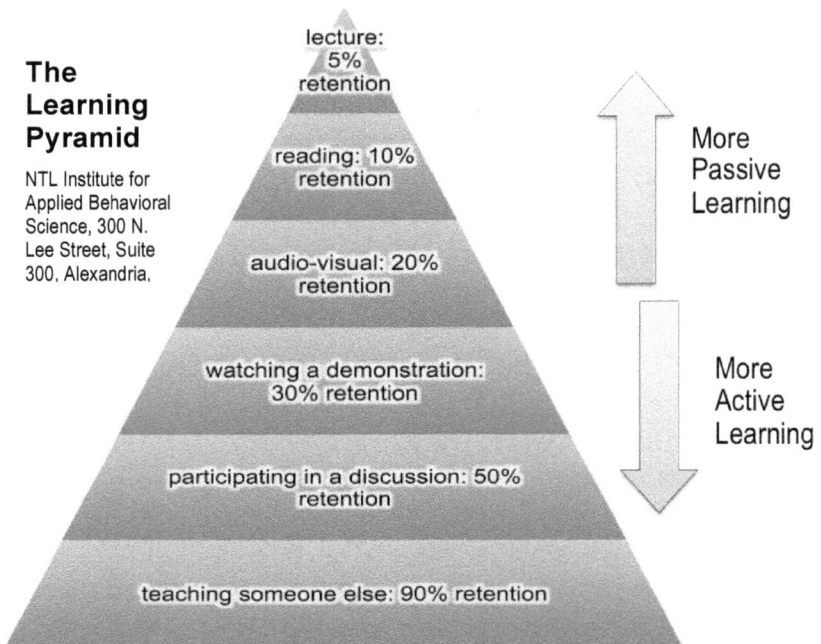

The Learning Pyramid

NTL Institute for Applied Behavioral Science, 300 N. Lee Street, Suite 300, Alexandria,

lecture: 5% retention

reading: 10% retention

audio-visual: 20% retention

watching a demonstration: 30% retention

participating in a discussion: 50% retention

teaching someone else: 90% retention

More Passive Learning

More Active Learning

Now the ideas in the learning pyramid indicate that the more a person participates is in their own learning, the more they retain. However, the way the learning pyramid describes what active learning is like has a verbal bias as well. Imagine for a moment that people can respond actively to information in any language they so choose. I myself am most fluent in speaking to through the language of paint, and so may respond back using this tongue. Other creative people may choose to respond using the vocabulary of dance, or music, or song. Some may choose to write words, versus speaking aloud. There are many ways to "participate in a discussion" in addition

—

to verbal dialogue. The point is that "participating in a discussion", particularly when having a discussion with the God who knows our hearts, can take the form of any expressive form. For myself as an artist, this knowledge comforts me, because I can rest in the knowledge that God understands me, even when what I have difficulty finding the words to express it.

I am so passionate about this because in my experience, often artists and other creative people get the message that they have talents of little importance. This is a travesty, because research clearly demonstrates the opposite. The body of Christ should allow people to worship God through each of these learning styles, and not force people into thinking that connection with God happens primarily through verbal means. Imagine how worship could be so much richer if all the ways that people learn were utilized in the church, and particularly in worship!

As it is, we are slowly beginning to see this transformation happen, but some days this seems like a very unhurried process. My fear is that the longer the church takes to embrace ideas like multiple learning styles in worship, the more people will be less able to connect to the church as a relevant institution in a world so filled with other messages that speak in these learning styles with such proficiency about things with much less substantive value.

—

But you, my friend, give me hope that you are trying to understand a person like me, a person who struggles to use words to explain to you how the visual helps me connect so movingly to God.

—

Why are we not worshiping together?

art as prayer

I rise up
in Your strength,
Father,
farther
than I ever have.
Open me.
In me
find
You.

Poem: "Lift" by Eric Nykamp, 2000

Exercise One: Understanding Your Unique Worship/ Learning Style

Looking at the "Learning to Remember" letter, consider which learning styles you use regularly. Since every person is created uniquely by God to serve a different purpose, it sometimes is important to attach language to these differences to understand and appreciate them better.

In the back of this book in Appendix 7, there are descriptions of the 7 primary worship/learning styles. Each of these styles is based on the Multiple Intelligences model of Howard Gardener. The reason to learn about these styles is simple: God has made us each with unique ways of understanding the world, and worshiping Him. If you want to take a diagnostic test, the website www.businessballs.com has a multiple intelligences test you can print and use[3]. So turn to the appendix and/or take this test, and see what your strengths are. Doing this will help you to unpackage the material in the next chapters better.

---

[3]
http://www.businessballs.com/freepdfmaterials/free_multiple_intelligences_test_manual_version.pdf

—

After you take the test, examine the ways you nurture your own Christian growth. Are you feeding your spiritual life through one or two styles… or many? Do you neglect feeding yourself spiritually through one of the styles you have affinity for, or do you worship in ways that focus on some styles more than others?

It is important to honor the way God made you and feed your spiritual growth in the styles you learn through best. You are not an accident. God made you to learn a certain way for a purpose. Don't wait for someone else to help you grow spiritually according to your learning style. Get creative and partner with God to deepen your spiritual walk in the ways you learn best! So think up ways, both verbal and non-verbal, that you can spend time with God. Write down your learning styles on a sheet of paper, and brainstorm several ways you can deepen your spiritual growth in the next year using your preferred styles. Once you are comfortable identifying your styles, remember to appreciate other people's styles that are different from yours. Learn to partner with people in your church community whose gifting is in different areas than yours. Become their friends. Love them. After all, God made us different for a purpose – to belong to each other, and love each other, just like God loved us in spite of our brokenness.

The following chapters are letters written from the perspective of a person with a visual-spatial style who sees the process of art making to be integral to the way he relates to God. As you read, notice how similar or different his style is from your own. As you look around

—

your own church community, see if this material helps you to understand these often-quiet people whose primary form of expression may be wordless or silent. Yet, God understands these wordless prayers, and if we love each other, we all must try to understand each other as well. Even if it is trying to learn a language without words.

—

part two –
the prayer of
the eye

I cannot stand up under this.

aesthetic prayer

Just as a body, though one,
has many parts, but all its
many parts form one body, so
it is with Christ.

I Corinthians 12:12

My friend, you asked me to help you learn how to
look at and understand art. So I have been
writing to you about learning how to think about
the role the non-verbal arts have played in
Christianity up until this point, because I believe
that understanding that there is some lost
understanding is foundational to relearning how
to understand art. We as Protestants,
collectively, have lost the ability to look at images
for the last 400 years from an imaginative
Christian standpoint. We have no collective
understanding of the symbolic language of the
church in many cases, and we in the church have
neglected our responsibility to foster a sense of
the presence of God in our daily life. Part of the
lost art of perceiving God is learning aesthetic,

—

non-verbal prayer, or as I like to call it – the prayer of the eye. I often think of this kind of prayer as "noticing" or "perceiving prayer."

I will be speaking as a visual artist here, though creative people from other disciplines may prefer to think of this kind of prayer as centered in another organ or part of the body. Dancers through their eyes notice motion, writers perceive through their eyes, ears, mouths and noses to describe many things. Musicians sense God through their ears. Whatever way you observe God in your own aesthetic language, this is the prayer of the eye.

Imagine, God created this amazing organ in the human body that collects images of reflected light, flips them upside down, and converts these sensations into electric signals · sending them through the nerves at the back of the eye to the brain where these impulses of energy are again analyzed and interpreted as forms, colors, and depth. This is not an accident – this is an organ created to know God as it understands the world He made and the creations of the creatures that inhabit it.

We in the church need to re-discover how to worship God with our eyes, as well as our whole bodies. We have neglected our bodily knowing of God for two long. I want to explore with you ways

—

that we can begin to develop this kind of knowing again.

Aesthetic prayer is a way of sensually understanding the world as a means by which God shows His goodness to us, makes us aware of our collective brokenness, and how God reveals Himself to us. It is a way of focusing on perceiving God through the five senses, or possibly just focusing on one sense, relishing and basking in a moment or an experience as if God created this one moment just to be with you. We come to hear and read about God through our ears and eyes, and speak to God through our mouths. Aesthetic prayer takes these same body parts and focuses them in a different way to understand and relate with God.

To illustrate this point further, imagine your entire body as a tablet on which God is writing a love letter to you. He may choose to write anywhere on your body, and at first writes with broad strokes over the entire surface of your body. But as He writes, he notices that when He touches certain areas of your body, that the ink seems to soak in to the tissue in certain places more than others, coloring the pigment of the skin like a tattoo applied to a sponge. These "receptive points" seem to soak in the message, and so God in his wisdom continues to write with focused attention in these more receptive areas of the body, allowing the message to permeate the

—

surface and with hope, penetrate the deepest part of your body with his love.

This is what it is like to be an artist – our "receptive points" seem to be somewhat different than other people we know. While some may be "ear sensitive", visual artists are "eye sensitive". The ear is no greater than the eye, nor the eye greater than the ear. Yet, in worship, often the language of the ear is given nearly exclusive prominence, which is a grave oversight in an increasingly visual culture. For artists, having the Gospel spoken in the language of the eye is critical to understanding the truth of the gospel. In addition, the more this sense is employed in worship, the more artists will be affirmed and recognize their way of communing with God. Being an artist is more than being a skillful arranger of paint or clay – it is about seeing God. And that, my friend, is something I want to share with you.

—

—

My God, I need you more than ever...

assumptive awareness

*But blessed are your eyes
because they see, and your
ears because they hear.
Truly I tell you, many
prophets and righteous
people longed to see what
you see but did not see it,
and to hear what you hear
but did not hear it.*

Matthew 13:16-17

The last time I wrote to you, I was telling you that I wanted to explain to you how artists see God. I meant that quite literally. Artists are trained to sharpen their perceptive skills much like a botanist is trained to differentiate between plan species or a doctor is trained to find abnormalities in the human body. Visual artists, first and foremost, know how to see.

That may seem unusual to you if you have never taken a drawing class. I remember my first drawing class. I wondered why we needed to take 3 hours to draw twice every week. I wondered what I would learn. What my drawing instructor taught was not only some techniques for rendering images, but primarily she taught me how to look at something for a very long time to see the beauty, complexity, and at times painfulness of the object on which I cast my gaze.

Now any person can be taught how to look, but not everyone can be taught how to see. Christians in particular have some advantages when it comes to seeing, though many of us do not sharpen our general awareness with our knowledge of God.

But what transforms the vision of the Christian is the awareness that God is here.

We need to assume this as Christians. I don't think that anyone would argue with me here. We profess that God made the world, that God is in the world, and that God is still active and working in the world (not floating up in space watching us scuttle about, disinterested and uninvolved). But what about assuming that we can sense God about us if we tune our eyes to see Him?

—

I call this idea "assumptive awareness". I think that as Christians, we do assume that God is about us at all times, and if we become aware of this, we realize that God is present even in the most ordinary experiences of our lives. Any idiot can sense the power of God in an earthquake, but it takes special vision to sense God in a grain of sand.

But assumptive awareness goes even further than this. Not only are we aware of God's presence, but we soon become aware that God is not passively present – He is actively reaching out to us and may choose any means by which to do so. He may even choose to communicate to us visually, if we have the eyes to see it.

This kind of artistic seeing is the core of what it means to be able to understand art. If we teach our eyes how to see God in the ordinary, searching for the way that God is trying to communicate with us, then it takes that same kind of seeing to look at a painting and see how God could communicate through that as well. However, I will tell you more about this in my next letter.

—

Oh God, my prayer is that we all may stop
thinking hateful things about each other and
just be what you called us to be – lovers of each other.

be still and know

He makes me lie down in
green pastures,
he leads me beside quiet
waters,

Psalm 23:2

I realized in my last letter that I neglected to tell
you something that happens when you learn to
see artistically. When you learn to see, you will
inadvertently learn the art of stillness.

I find that the two most sacred environments that
I can think of are church buildings and art
museums. Both of these spaces are quiet when
empty, and I always image the people that seem
to embody the emptiness. In the empty church, I
imagine the many words spoken and the many
bodies that have filled the seats in that room over
time. I recall the roar of full-throated worship,
and the silent tears that have fallen to the floor
over the years. In the museum, I imagine the

—

artists whose spirits are somehow still present in the works they left behind. I have a sense of the rainbow of emotions that have been stroked into each painting which hang on the walls. In both spaces, I feel a sense of being known. In the church, I feel that my soul is understood, and in the museum, my artistic nature feels accepted as normal in this quiet place that respects and holds this part of myself sacred. Interestingly, in both these places, I get a deep sense of the presence of God.

I was telling you about that first drawing class that I had as a student in college. I wondered what would happen in the 3-hour period that I had devoted to drawing. Something happens to the human body when we focus our attention. The class would start, and people would be chatting away, music playing low in the background. But within an hour, the room was silent, hands moving, capturing the image of the model or still life on paper. We became mentally still, and were learning to see God.

My friend, if you try to see God through your eyes in this way, you too may come to discover the wonder of this kind of stillness. There is something wonderful that happens when we focus and reflect. It is this kind of openness to sensing God that I believe the psalmist wrote of in Psalm 131:

—

"I do not concern myself with great matters or things too wonderful for me. But I have stilled and quieted my soul..."

Just as holy people for centuries have meditated on the words of scripture, visual artists meditate on the book of God written throughout the visual world around us. Only many of us fail to see it through eyes immersed in the knowledge that we are continually in the presence of a holy God. But when our eyesight is transformed in this way, it is a truly wonderful realization. I hope you can experience this some day for yourself as you learn to see God about you, as well as in art.

—

You pour into me once and over.

anticipative observing

Whoever has ears to hear, let them hear.

Luke 8:8b

I am still learning to look with anticipation for God. There are days like today, when the sky is overcast and rain is drizzling down, that it is hard for me to imagine God being everywhere present. I imagine God so often to be associated with light that it is difficult to see God in the darkness, but it is possible · even though it is difficult.

I hope that by now you are beginning to learn not only how to see God, but also developing a sense of expectancy that you *will* see God. This is a habit that takes years to foster. I have heard some of my elders talk about the fact that the older they get the more effortless this becomes, at least in some respects. I had one friend, the artist Jim Fissel, tell me that he has difficulty sleeping at night. He often wakes up at 4:30 in the morning because the symptoms of his

—

Parkinson's disease cause his sleep to be disrupted. Now he could be angry with God that this disease is taking a toll on his body and robs him of sleep. I imagine he has some days like this. But instead, he has come to find God in these still hours of the morning. He says that the only other person up at that time is God, so they spend time together · painting. He is anticipating the day that he will be with God in Heaven, and is developing the awareness of Him in these last days while he is still on earth. That is the kind of relationship that I find enhanced by this kind of visual prayer – a deeper awareness that God is with us always. I am learning to anticipate that God is going to communicate visually with me. I look forward to seeing where my attention is drawn naturally, and am learning to wonder what God could be saying to me there. I am developing a habit of seeing God.

This hit me again this weekend. I was visiting with friends, and we were talking about things that remind us of how God works. The conversation drifted to things, symbolic objects, which we have in our homes that remind us of God. Some of these reminders were quite literal, like crosses and framed Bible verses, but other people had less obvious reminders: bowels, plants, handmade objects. These things I found more interesting because they engaged the imagination. It took me a minute, but then I realized that I too had things in my home that similarly reminded me of God.

I collect Yixing teapots, a kind of "purple clay" that ranges in color from light terra cotta to a charcoal black color. These small, Chinese teapots, fit in the palm of the hand and are crafted by artisans and fired raw with no glaze, allowing the natural colors of the clay to be exposed. In talking with my friends, I realized that it was not just the artistic beauty of these teapots that held my fascination; it was also the way that these small pieces of art were like people.

These teapots are designed to be used with loose-leaf teas, boiling water poured into the pots to wash, then steep the tealeaves. But the exposed clay of the pots also adds a richness to the flavor of the tea, and with repeated uses the flavor enhancing qualities of the clay becomes stronger and stronger. In many ways, these teapots remind me of the Christian life. Each of us is individually shaped by our creator God to be beautiful in our own right, and God pours himself into us – washing us and filling us. However, like the tea in the pot, being filled by God does little good unless we pour ourselves out to share with others, and open ourselves to be used over and over in this way. For me, teapots remind me of my relationship with God.

The idea of seeing something of God in the everyday is not a new idea. In fact, it is a very Biblical one. Many of Jesus' parables took everyday things from common Hebrew life and used them as metaphors for the Christian life. By doing this, he gradually created a landscape where the common things that surrounded people from that culture because visual reminders of God. Seeds, sheep, trees, water, fish, light, darkness – all these things and many more because powerful visual reminders of God. This is the parable principle – re-casting the everyday landscape into a visual reminder of God.

Could this be one of the roles visual artists, writers, and lyricists could play in this present culture? Could this be something all creative people could do to transform whatever culture they find themselves in? Would this not enliven sermons, stories, and the spiritual life? I think it would. But wherever any of us are, fostering this kind of readiness to commune with God through whatever means he chooses to commune with us is a wonderful thing. To be with God, all we need to do is be ready open, and aware in our everyday lives.

I hope that you are also learning to find God in the hidden everyday places in your life. I pray that God gently takes hold of your imagination and transforms your vision so that your everyday world becomes a visual reminder of God. This is my prayer for you: that as this develops and

—

becomes a habit in your life, that you become aware that your eyes are watching God - everywhere.

If you
remain silent.   Psalm 28:1

reflective perceiving

The heavens declare the
glory of God;
the skies proclaim the work
of his hands.

Psalm 19:1

I have been writing to you all this time about learning to see, and by seeing somehow entering into an awareness of the presence of God, training our eyes to see God about us. This is my one hope – that people learn to see God. When we learn to see God, it is hard to experience so much doubt. Our culture teaches us to doubt, especially to doubt the existence of God or doubt in His care for us. And yet, there are those who can see God in the most powerful to the most insignificant details of life. We see God's fingerprints in the stuff of everyday life. We know He is here, and even when we cannot understand Him, we know that He loves us.

—

But what good is seeing if there is no thinking to follow. I mean this quite literally. If all we learn to do is see God, but this vision does not prompt us to ask questions, we have not grown in our faith. No, something needs to happen in our prayer life that is transformative when we pray visually with God. We need to begin questioning.

I heard a speaker once who made the comment that one of the primary values of works of visual art is the fact that art makes us ask questions. This question-prompting vision is what is very dearly needed in the Christian community. We have so often lost a sense of the mystery of God, we do not often ponder the kinds of things that cause us to wonder about the unknowable. And yet, there is something very important about these kinds of musings. I believe that asking questions about what we see, particularly with the mindset that God is setting these visual "calls to prayer" all about us all day, is needed for Christian growth.

Let me give you two examples from my own life. One of the pastors at my church formerly was a biology professor. With her background, the natural world is rippling with metaphors informed by her knowledge of science. She cannot look at a flower without appreciating it as a scientist. Similarly, my father, who was a carpenter and woodworker his entire life, cannot help but look at a building or piece of furniture without also imagining the steps it would take to craft it. The

—

point of this is that we all carry with us different kinds of knowledge from our education and life experiences and the arts that we can use to inform our viewing and with which we can develop further questions. We all are the people God made us to be. Who we have been created to be impacts the way we understand our vision. We should not hide from that.

With this kind of informed viewing, every walk we take becomes a visual prayer with God. Every moment in our homes becomes an opportunity to be with God. Every journey is a call to attention to see –literally – that God is here. We only need to ponder what it is that He wants us to think about today as you spend time together.

—

Offering

meditative recording

See, I have chosen
Bezalel son of Uri, the son
of Hur, of the tribe of
Judah, and I have filled
him with the Spirit of God,
with wisdom, with
understanding, with
knowledge and with all kinds
of skills— to make artistic
designs...

Exodus 31:2-4a

There is a critical difference between an appreciator and a practitioner. I have been writing to you about how to pray with your eyes, but what I am about to tell you is the final step in learning to pray visually – a step that will take you from being a person who prays at a distance to someone who has entered the inner courts of intimacy with our creator God. This step takes

—

you from appreciating God's handiwork to responding with the work of your own hands – completing the cycle of visual communication by responding back in your own non-verbal language. This is meditative recording.

Let me explain by going back to a story about my father. I previously told you that my father was, and still is, a carpenter. I have many memories and stories that come from being around him while he worked on projects. I spent time growing up playing in the sawdust, tinkering with hammers, and watching many things being made that came from my dad's imagination. I was not gifted in such a way to take naturally to these same tools, but from being around so much woodworking equipment, I can appreciate a good piece of furniture from a piece that is not well-made. My appreciation is informed, but it is not the appreciation of someone who knows first-hand how to craft a piece of furniture. I could not even begin to replicate a cabinet that my father has made, though I have watched him do this many times myself. My hands are not familiar with the process. My body does not know what my eyes appreciate.

But when I walk into an art museum, I am surrounded by paintings, many of which speak to me and some of which I will get very close to in order to see how exactly is the paint on the surface of the canvas was manipulated to create the image that strikes me... and I may go home

———

afterwards and give it a try myself. And that is the critical difference. With the cabinet, I respond by appreciating the one who made it. But I respond to the painting by creating one myself. To pray visually means to communicate visually back to God the way that God has communicated visually with you.

Now for many of us, inspiration comes directly from nature, or even from the creations of the people whom God has created to fill the earth. Both the creations of people and God are wonderful, and we may choose to respond back through the limited means of pencil, paint, film, wood, clay or other means of creating art. I am speaking of responding back visually. For some of us, our responses may take the forms of words, dance, or sound, but for the sake of consistency, let me stick with the visual examples here. I think that something profound happens when we are so moved by something that we feel the need to respond back. I think that this is something very natural that so often we lose as we grow into adulthood. In his famous book, The Little Prince, Antoine DeSaint-Exupery describes how this happened for him after finding that his drawings, which were so meaningful to him, were not understood by the adults he showed them to. He writes, "The grown-ups advised me to put away my drawings... and apply myself instead to geography, history, arithmetic, and grammar. That is why I abandoned, at the age of six, a magnificent career as an artist. I had been discouraged by the failure of my drawing..." As we grow into adolescents, we stifle our spontaneous desire to respond freely to things so as not to stand out, only to realize later as adults that we have lost something intrinsic to being a person – to relate through our senses together. We often continue to live "adult" lives preoccupied with a fear of what people may think of us, and settle for a life of safe banality. How empty life becomes when we lose the joy of unencumbered expression!

Artists know something important about God that many of the rest of us have forgotten. We record our journey through life in a language without words, the images of which populate our sketchbooks like a prayer journal. But upon reflection, these images possess the ability to both stun us with their beauty, while reminding us of the times we have walked with God, and stand as an aesthetic witness of our aesthetic journey with God through the pain and glory of life.

Now this is important. Yes, it is important to get some "nice pictures" when we respond visually to God, but there is something of more value that transpires during the still times of image making. We pour out our hearts to God. And the record of these times of outpouring chronicles something important about the Christian life.

———

Each of these memories is drawn out – literally. Yes, I said memory. Because what an artist renders is not just the actual look of a thing – it somehow captures an aspect of the experience of looking, communicated through the artists' personal style. Trees do not "really" look like they are created out of pencil lead, and buildings to not "really" appear as they do on shiny, photo paper. People do not look like they are made of marble, and however powerful a moving image is on a television screen, life is not made of tiny digital specks of colored light turning on and off. The very act of rendering something changes it, but it is also a way for us to capture the experience that we as renders have. We capture what stands out to us as important.

And what seems important at one moment in time can change when we look back in retrospect. This is where art-making as a form of prayer takes on an interesting dynamic.

Theoretically, the work of art captures the artist's experience – freezing it for all eternity. But for the artist, the image is not just an objective rendering, but also an emotional one. Like art, the brain captures memories through an emotional lens, cataloguing experiences by the emotional charges that they carry. This is known as mood-congruent memory. This is the reason that when people feel blue, that they seem to be able to only think of times in their lives that things have been terrible. It is also the reason

—

that when people feel sunny inside that life seems as if everything has always been grand. By reviewing our artwork, we will have recorded visual prayers to God during the good times and the bad, and these creations can stand as a reminder that God has never left us or forsaken us. He is always with us through it all. Our art will, over time, literally put this fact before our eyes. And since these experiences are frozen for all eternity, we will be able to view each others works of art and know that we are not alone, that others have walked this way before us and like the cloud of witnesses, we can know that God will walk with us as He walked with them.

I hope that you now can see, or at least understand, how to think of a work of art that you encounter. I hope you learn to pray with your eyes, to companion with God. I hope that your seeing becomes transformed the way your heart is, and that this process of transforming continues every day.

But there is one more thing that I want you to know, though I have started to tell you about it already. But I will save this for another letter.

Exercise Two: Noticing Prayer

In this section, we examined how God's presence surrounds us, similar to the way water surrounds fish. This next exercise is designed to heighten your awareness of God's presence in our daily lives, by learning to notice all the evidence of God that we so often overlook because we are not attentive to it.

So this exercise requires that we put a premium on removing anything that could be potentially distracting and putting it away for the duration of this exercise. For example, if having a cell phone or music player is potentially distracting to your thought process, it would be a good idea to turn them off or leave them somewhere safe while you take time to learn this kind of noticing prayer.

Here is the exercise: Take a walk for at least 30 minutes or more, being mindful of noticing signs of God's presence all around you. You may find it helpful to take a camera or sketchbook along with you to record what you notice. With this mindset, ease into this way of sensing God around you. Sometimes when in this frame of mind, God has our attention and may communicate something to you. Note these things and share them with a trusted friend whose spiritual discernment you respect.

After your walk, reflect on what you noticed, possibly discussing this with a group if this exercise is done with a retreat group or other small group. Some people may find that writing a prayer back to God or drawing about this experience may be a powerful way to remember this moment.

———

part three –
the prayer of
the hand

I list you

artistic prayer

Look to the LORD and his
strength;
seek his face always.

Psalm 105:4

In my last letter, I hinted that there was
something more that I needed to tell you about
visual prayer. What I wanted to share with you is
how the art-making process itself is a form of
prayer. I want you to join me in shifting focus
from a "looking" perspective to a "doing"
perspective, to change from praying with your
eyes to praying with your body.

For myself, I think of art making prayer as the
"prayer of the hand". In this form of prayer, I
conceptualize my hand and paintbrush as I would
my lips in spoken prayer. My hand articulates my
heart. For writers and musicians, our hands do
the majority of our praying, though dancers and
actors may mind that it is easier to think of this

as "body prayer". When I lead drum circles, I will often tell the drummers assembled about how drumming in the presence of God is similarly a form of prayer. I will say something like this, "I want you to take whatever feeling you have in your heart and put it into your hands. Now take your hands, and play that feeling on your drum, creating a rhythm that we will send straight to the ear of God. God knows what is in our hearts, even when we cannot express it with words." However, for the sake of consistency, I am going to speak as an artist and will refer to this kind of prayer as the "prayer of the hand."

Artistic prayer, at its core, is prayer-by-making, the kind of prayer that only becomes deep the longer you are at it. A work of art, while it is being made, is a prayer in progress, the kind of interactive, conversational prayer between the artist and God. Only once the work is completed does it take on a new life as an object prompting a reflective, "prayer of the eye" which I have been writing to you about. In this letter (and those that follow), I will not be talking with you about finished products. I will be talking about unfinished artwork, which is in the process of being made.

 All artists are trying to express an idea, be it a simple one or a highly complex one. But the work of art is a process that is not worked out ahead of time. Rather, it is the interaction between the artist and the materials being worked with. God

———

joins us in this struggle, communicating with us through manipulating paint, brushing ink, moving pencils, shaping clay, carving stone, cutting wood, using a computer, or framing an image in a viewfinder. The interaction between the artist and the material is one of the many ways that the artist can perceive the still, small voice of God. It is this very interaction with materials, which forms the vocabulary of artistic prayer.

Artists, always seeing and perceiving, may find these interchanges between the material and the spiritual to be one way this kind of communion with God takes place. Often our frustration with a technical problem gives us new ideas for how to render the idea we are trying to express. Other times, wrestling with mastery over a material teaches us things about ourselves as people – how to handle our emotions, or even causes us to reflect on how we are like the material we are struggling to control. Then there are times when compositional difficulties cause us to consider new solutions to our visual problems, often requiring us to be reflective (almost prayerful in approach) so as to see the possible answers.

Let me give you an example from my own recent experience. I have been particularly concerned recently for a friend of mine who has been battling depression for five years. I was not aware of how serious this battle had become until the past few weeks when he told me that he was thinking about taking his own life. So he has understandably been on my mind. I too struggle with depression, but my lows are not as deep, nor as long, as his. I did not realize how much his story was affecting me until I noticed that I was drawing images in my sketchbook of a falling figure. This image was a powerful one for me, and I drew it over and over again, refining it, working it over, contemplating it. My sketches revealed that my heart was crying for my friend. I decided to paint this idea as a way to more formally pray for him.

Over the next few weeks, while he sought treatment, I spent time with him, and also spent time alone, painting. My painting time was my time to be quiet with God, the God who knew my heart and how I felt about my friend. As with my sketches, I painted the figure, changing colors, shapes, details until I felt that my image of a falling woman captured as best as I could render the sentiments that swirled in my heart. But there was this empty space around my falling woman, space that seemed to me to want to be filled by something... but by what?

This visual problem called to me. I felt that what I put in this space around the falling figure would somehow complete the emotion I was wrestling with. I waited, which is difficult at times for me to do. I did not want to just put something in the space just to fill it so I could move on to another piece. I chose to sit with the discomfort of this emptiness that was in front of me. Eventually, the answer came quietly to my mind. Butterflies.

In my mind, I could see this woman falling into a cloud of flittering butterflies, which seemed to hold her, pillowing her, catching her fall. This juxtaposition of falling and lifting, heaviness and lightness, a fragile person plummeting and the quiet flittering insects cradling her spoke to me that my friend was being cared for by God. So I painted, with joy, the finishing touches to my piece... and now have let it rest. Complete.

As I am typing these words, this piece is next to me in my art studio where I am writing on my laptop. I don't know what will happen in my friend's life. But I know that I have a God who is there, with all of us, whom I can speak to with the prayers of my hands.

———

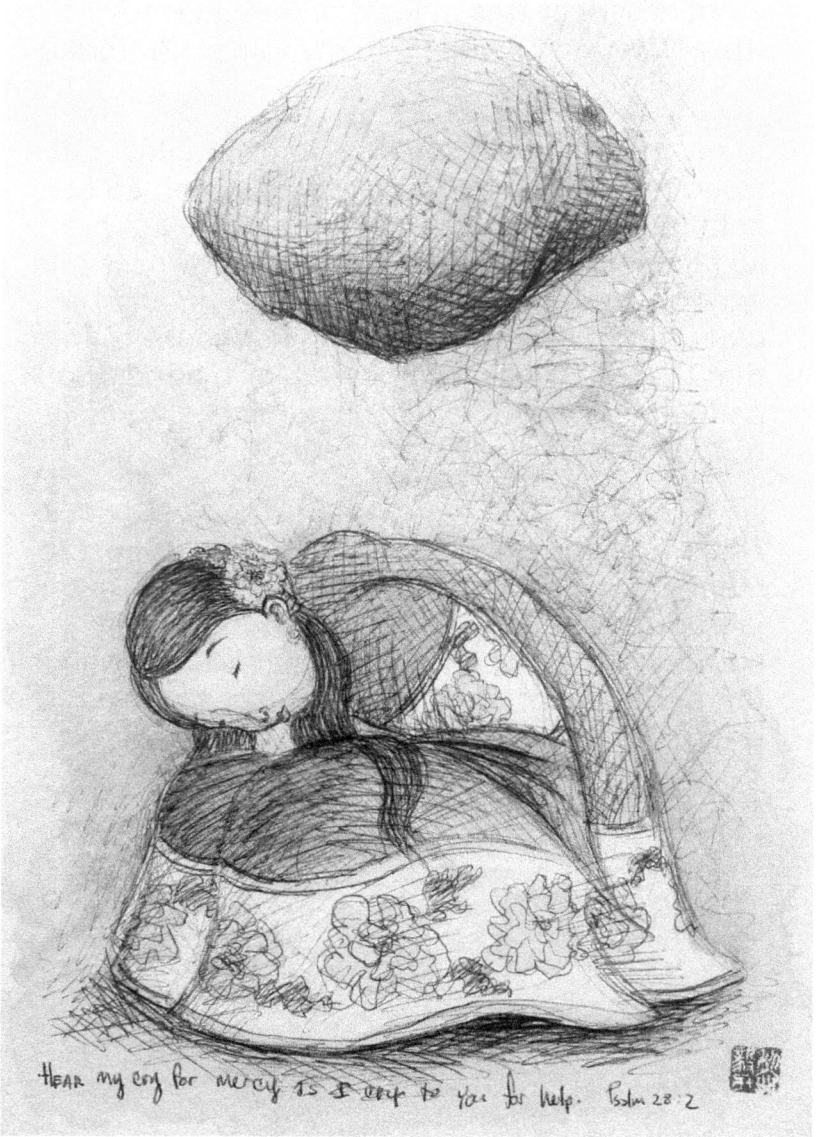

HEAR my cry for mercy as I cry to you for help. Psalm 28:2

the aesthetic chapel

"Do not come any closer,"
God said. "Take off your
sandals, for the place where
you are standing is holy
ground."

Exodus 3:5

As I write to you today, I am so deeply aware of
the prayerful state of art making. I wish I could
let you experience with me the kind of inner silent
state that happens while creating. I had a
moment like this yesterday when I lost track of all
time and my hand was just fixed on making the
painting I was working on, allowing my mind the
freedom to wander, allowing me to reflect on my
life. These reflections helped me to clarify
struggles I was having, and gave me the
awareness of how I was feeling to be able to
clearly talk about these things with my wife later
in the evening.

I have a place that I can go to when I need to pray. This is my aesthetic chapel, my sanctuary where I return to commune with my creator God. I want to tell you about this place.

My chapel is my art studio, a room above my garage, a spacious room with a wooden floor; walls sloped in from the sides from the peak of the roof, walls painted a pear-green. There is one window, facing south (I wish I had north light, but this cannot be helped). I hope to hang a paper shade over the window soon to diffuse the light. There are bookcases along one wall, and I have a small radio sitting on top of a drum I carried back with me from Liberia. Along with a desk I have had since childhood and an old leather chair is my easel and paints sitting inside an old roll-top desk. A large paper lantern hangs from the ceiling, and I have a tall spotlight that I move freely about the room at will. On top of the bookcases are piles of CD's, some African sculptures, and some Chinese teapots, chops, and ink-making supplies. A rag-rug from India covers the back portion of the room, breaking up the visual space of the room. On this rug my two young daughters come to play on many a Saturday afternoon when they wake from their naps to find me in the "painting room". This is a room of music, creativity, and at times – silence and light. This is the place where I meet God. This is my aesthetic chapel.

The few feet in front of my easel are the most holy ground I have in my house. It is here that I am most likely to be aware of being in the presence of God.

Now, not everyone has the luxury of having a studio in his or her home. For a while, I had to paint in my dining room, and then found my working space in a series of bedrooms that my wife and I shared. But any place can be a place of aesthetic prayer so long as there are some common elements.

An aesthetic chapel needs to be a place suited to the kind of art that you want to create, a room that does not by its structure impede your creative work. Not that any space will be perfect. The chapel of my studio has a south-facing window, the light sometimes streaming in hot and harsh. But the idea is that the room is not too hot or cold, that there is enough space for your body to move the way that you want to work, and hopefully in a location where you can visit it often without much delay.

I should say here that my studio is in my home, which could be a dangerous place for some people to work. I have many artist friends who need to have a space outside of their home so that they can come home and focus only on their family without the temptation to go back in to the studio to work. However, for me, renting a studio space is not reasonable at this time, as it would not be for many others as well.

An aesthetic chapel also needs to be a place where work can lay out, ideally where it can be left undisturbed. This is difficult for many of us who live in small spaces, who may have to consider mobility issues, or have small children who may tinker with anything they find laying out. However, we are speaking idealistically here. Ideally, this would be how an aesthetic chapel should function. After all, if God is speaking to us visually, having our in-progress art out where we can see it allows God to have this conversation with us any time we even enter His space.

Realistically, however, it is unlikely that many of us will be able to have spaces where we can leave our inspiring, creative clutter out for long. Sooner or later, we must tidily put away our things and return to a sense of order. But, what is more important is that we return to the same space to work creatively, building up layers of artistic experiences in the same place over and over. This patina of creative activity soon will transform this space in your mind from a room, desk, or seat to a holy and God-saturated place.

I have a friend who does her devotions every day while sitting on the far left cushion of her couch in her apartment. I can't help but think about this seat as the place where she meets God, every time I visit her. This is her holy spot. My holy space is the six square feet in front of my easel, where the light of God showers my imagination every time I stand there, clicking on my floodlight to signal my time to begin.

Wait for the Lord
be strong and take heart
and wait for the Lord

alternate sanctuaries

Now when Daniel learned
that the decree had been
published, he went home to
his upstairs room where the
windows opened toward
Jerusalem. Three times a
day he got down on his
knees and prayed, giving
thanks to his God, just as
he had done before.

Daniel 6:10

I was thinking of you the other day after I was
reading over this last letter. It seems to me that
while there is something particularly unique
about having a creative space as part of an
experiential way to know God, it is by no means
the only way. In fact, an experiential, reflective
practice can be had through many activities and

in many places, a studio space being only one special kind.

It is important, however that these kind of reflective spiritual practices take place in environments that lend themselves to introspection. This means that the space has to be conducive to mental wandering. I am coming more and more to believe that the moments in which I am closest to God are the times many would consider that I am "wasting time". That is a good thing. Maybe other cultures are different, but in my urban, technological and highly stimulating world, there are few things that have not been streamlined and organized by someone else so that I can be more efficient with my time. Whenever I hear the word "efficient", I think of the word "busier". Efficient people are busy all time, and their attention is so poured into task-completion that we have lost as a culture the ability to daydream. The fact is, we have lost something when we are so busy, something that engagement in creative activity restores. All of us need to let our minds wander off the leash, lest we become snappish, grumpy dogs.

But often, creative activity contains within it an element of sensual, bodily engagement. It allows our bodies to be busy, allowing our minds to fly free. When searching for an alternate sanctuary in which to reflect on God, look for spaces in which you too can busy your body in an activity that allows you to think of other things.

———

I suggest, that all of us need to have a sensual, physical spiritual practice with which to balance our cerebral understanding of God, bridging fully the distance between the head and the heat. This kind of "knowing God" can balance our theological "knowing about God" and help all of us develop a holistic, spiritual Christian practice. If you cannot find a desk, dance floor, or studio in which to meet with God, consider having a standing date with God in one of the following places:

If you are inside your home, think of different rooms where you may meet God. It is quite possible that some of these rooms are holy spaces for you as well.

Let's start with the bathroom. Ok, I know that this is probably not the kind of thing you were expecting to read on a book on art and the spiritual life, but take a step back and consider objectively the spiritual significance of this room. The bathroom is where we go to be alone, get clean, where we stand naked in the presence of God alone, where we see our reflection, where we go when we feel sick. It is a place where we leave behind our waste and dirt, and where we go to cleanse ourselves and take medicine when we need to be healed. It is the place where we scrutinize ourselves and where we go to make ourselves presentable. The bathroom is the room most associated with humility, transformation, and weakness. This can be a powerful place to meet God.

The bedroom too can be a sacred space. The bedroom is a place of privacy, a place of intimacy and passion, a place where passions can also flare. Our beds are places where we are most likely to be still in the dark of night, listening only to the sounds of the sleeping world and the ramblings of our thoughts. Our beds are also places where marital relationships find their most succinct non-verbal expression. The bedroom is the place in which people most likely keep their most private and precious items – diaries, photos, mementos, jewelry, clothing etc. The bedroom is associated with relationships and memories, as well as quiet. What kind of relationship could you have with God in this sanctuary?

Gathering rooms and public places in your home are other special spaces, be it inside or outside the structure of the home. Dining rooms, family rooms, sitting rooms, parlors, front porches and back patios are all places where people gather to share food, company, and conversation. When empty, the sight of vacant chairs and wider spaces can allow us to get in touch with our inner selves. These are rooms associated with the important relationships in our lives. What does God want to talk to you about the relationships in your life?

The kitchen is the one room in every home devoted to the act of creation. It is also another room associated with intimacy. It is a space where people linger, become curious, or talk while working. This is the space closest to the art-studio found in every home. Special foods, ordinary foods, comfort foods, and exotic dishes are created here. Memories especially associated with smells and tastes are made here, and this is the room in which there is much business. Again, this is a space devoted to creating and cleaning, a place filled with tools and gadgets. Washing dishes and doing other repetitive tasks can be opportunities for meditation and reflection, invaluable spiritual activities for anyone involved in this act of culinary creativity.

The shop, office, or den is another interesting spiritual space. It is often the place of work, where problems are solved, frustrations are fueled, and solutions are found to the very things that once were so frustrating. It is a place where we are literally working "on" something, a place that too can remind us of how God works on us.

Cleaning a home is another spiritual experience, a time in which the repetitions of cleaning motions allow us to fix our physical energies while releasing the imagination to explore many other things. Sweeping, scrubbing, vacuuming, polishing, sorting, organizing, and throwing away are all activities with metaphoric spiritual significance, as well as generally busy activities that allow us time to let our thoughts wander.

Working in a garden, doing repetitive exercise, walking, or chopping wood also are activities done in and around the home which similarly allow us to think while keeping our bodies busy.

But what is special about the artist's studio builds on the strengths of all these other sanctuaries. In the studio, the body is busy but the mind is free as well. But artistic business has one defining characteristic that sets it apart. The business of artistic expression intrinsically is communication back to the giver of the ideas, a give-and-take relationship of response to the visual product in front of the artist – a visual prayer (or interchange) with God. And this interchange, my friend, is what makes the prayer of the hand so special to me.

Release

the rhythm of creation

I am the true vine, and my
Father is the gardener. He
cuts off every branch in me
that bears no fruit, while
every branch that does bear
fruit he prunes so that it will
be even more fruitful.

John 15:1-2

Imagine a gardener who dreams of a garden full
of beautiful flowers and vegetables. He buys
seeds, plants them, and waters the soil only to
return to his home, shower off the dirt, and spend
the rest of the growing season watching television
while his garden parches under the beaming
summer sun. He occasionally gets up,
remembers his dream of a lush garden, and
unwinds the hose, spraying a light mist of water
over the now sandy soil, but then returns to watch
television. At harvest time, he walks at dusk to
the dusty patch of dry dirt, muttering to himself

that his seeds must be to blame because he has no plants to harvest, no vegetables to eat, and no flowers to cut with which to dress his table. Frustrated, he kicks at the grit, walks to the house, unties his boots, and returns to the well-indented sofa where he turns on the television and minutes later has forgotten all about his dreams for a garden. There his sits, eyes fixed and motionless, arms limp, mouth half-open, sedated and anesthetized, appearing to resemble the parched plants that have withered in his own, neglected garden.

Many of us expect our creative lives to be like the un-watered garden. We dream our creative dreams, but have not the discipline to do what is needed. We are like drummers who randomly strike our drumheads, surprised that we are not creating a beat with which we can dance. What we need, is a creative rhythm.

Creating a creative rhythm is something that must be thought out, unlike our ideas, which often come spontaneously without much effort. This is the structure in which we can create. This is discipline. I was talking with an artist friend recently who talked about this. He said "I usually like to think outside the box, but I created this box in which I put myself, thereby giving myself permission to create anywhere within it." I could not agree more.

———

There are some common elements to the rhythm of creation that are the same for everyone who creates. Let me briefly explore these ideas here.

The first is that every artist needs a creative tempo. We need to anticipate when we will be able to create next so as to be able to function well in our busy lives. There needs to be a regular pattern to our creative periods, frequent intervals that allow us to give habitual expression to our imaginations. It is like eating. If we eat without regularity, we will either become obese (eating whenever we like) or will starve (eating infrequently). Good dietary habits take structure to maintain, and like most of the best things in life will not happen unless we put forth the effort to make time for them.

The second is that we also need to have an expected duration of time in which we can create, so as to budget our creative time. I use the word budget intentionally, as this is an apt metaphor here. I need to know how to appropriate my limited time. If my creative time is my moment with God, I want to define the boundaries of this moment so that I can appreciate it while it lasts. Knowing what to expect allows me to appreciate it while it exists.

This expectation is like a flower. Every season around my house, the flowers begin quietly blooming according to their little timers, which start ticking after a push from the first warming light of spring. At the moment the snow recedes, the snowdrops and crocuses push themselves through the soil and pop open and inch or two above the surface. The flowers open and close up until the last warm day of early fall when the stonecrop and chrysanthemums stubbornly defy the coming cold. Every couple of weeks during the warm season, different flowers open, blessing my eyes with the points of color that catch my attention for the week or two that they are in bloom. Sure, I wish that the petals could remain open for longer than a few days, but that is part of their beauty, it is part of what I appreciate about them. They are beautiful while they last, but then I look forward to their return again next season. I know that each variety of flowers will be in bloom for a week or two, and I know what to expect during the moment that I have with them. The same principle holds true for my time creating with God in my studio. For the hour or two that I have in front of my easel, I appreciate that time. Yes, I wish that I could paint for many hours straight like I did when I was a student. But I am not a student now, and I must come to accept that my present circumstances do not allow for this kind of time right now. Maybe someday I will have more time again, or it could be just as likely that some day I will look back and feel that this period in my life and wish for it to return. All we have is right now, and we can choose to spend it wishing, or spend it working. No, it is important to know how much time you

—

can devote to art-making each time you create, so as to anticipate your own creative rhythm.

The third element of creating this rhythm is to abstain from distraction. In my life right now this is a tall order. As I write, in my studio is a playpen filled with toys, a child's drum and other musical toys, a pile of kids books, my wife's computer and desk, as well as my stereo and creative clutter. When I am painting, the chances that I will be able to paint uninterrupted are slim. However, the general atmosphere in my art studio is that this is a quiet room. My three-year old understand this now. When she enters the room after taking a nap, she often gives me a hug, we have a brief chat and I see if she needs to have her diaper changed. But after that, we both resume some quiet creative time, she drawing with her crayons, I painting at my easel. My one-year old, however, does not appreciate this time, but she will. For now, I am learning to juggle her in one arm while painting with the other if she needs my attention while I am creating.

But generally speaking, these are times that I try as best I can to abstain from distraction, even if this means that I only can have this kind of focus for a little while. I love the times when it is still in my studio, be it on a bright and sunny afternoon or in the dark of night late into the evening. When I am able to find a moment of calm, I am so much better able to busy my body so I can focus

—

on other things. These are the times when I am able to pray as an artist.

These are the elements that make up a creative rhythm. Like the way that church-going people return weekly for services in their houses of worship, so also do artists need to regularly visit our creative sanctuaries to spend time in communion with the creator God. We need our creative Sabbath. It is what we need to stay spiritually and artistically healthy. It is the way that God created our spiritual stomachs to feel full once again.

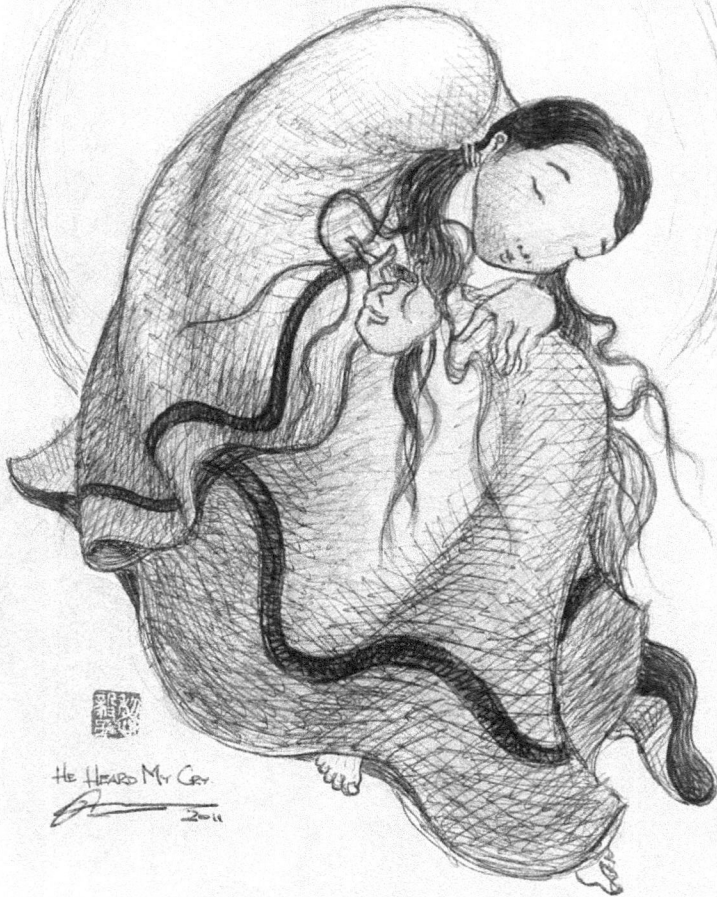

He Heard My Cry.

the artist's prayer

A discerning person keeps
wisdom in view,
but a fool's eyes wander to
the ends of the earth.

Proverbs 17:24

So now I hope that you understand somewhat
better about how to look at a piece of art and
understand what it means. I must confess that
even as an artist, I do not understand every work
of art, just as I do not understand the ways of
God even though I have been a Christian all of my
life. There is more to art than understanding.
Sometimes to understand art, you must live with
it for a while first.

It is my prayer for you that you do not become
frustrated and give up on trying to let a piece of
art speak to you when you do not immediately
understand what it "means". We live in a time
that has been stripped of mystery, wonder, and

reflection. Visual art asks us to resurrect these lost arts within ourselves. Visual art often is a prayer without words, the "groans" of the spirit that only God can fully understand, but which we can understand in part.

So what makes these artistic expressions valuable? How can looking at a work of art lead to deeper spiritual growth? I think in many ways the answer to these questions cannot come from deductive reasoning, because artwork is not designed to be understood this way. Art is not logic, science, or theology. It is not even illustration, which is dependant on words in all cases. It stands on its own and can only be understood on its own terms – through the arts of wonder and reflection. To use a Biblical parallel, works of visual art are less like the book of Romans, and more like the book of Psalms.

Truly understanding art is like trying to convince someone of the existence of God. You can talk about God all you want, but unless you talk "to" God, you have no way to truly experience Him. The same goes for understanding art. Art can only be understood when we take time with it. It is valuable because it is created by one of God's children, whom He loves and who He loves to see creating just as He is a creator. It is important because works of art are (knowingly or unknowingly) visual prayers to God, a cry from the heart of the artist to the heart of God. It is precious because God collects all of our prayers and sentiments like tears in a jar. Similarly, the walls of our churches and galleries can become glimpses into just a few of these tears. Art is vital because it begs us to keep our abilities to perceive the hints and whispers of His presence sharp and aware. Art asks us to remain alert to God, training our eyes to see Him and our hands to know Him.

Often when I do not understand a work of art, I want to blame the artist. This is ironic since I myself am an artist. This is only my frustration. I need to steady myself, remembering that God understands me even when I am unclear. I need to concentrate on the fact that God completely understands what this art means, just as He understands the person who made it.   And if God understands, it is not my place to blame the artist for the fact that I do not understand, it is my place to ask God to open my eyes so that I can see in part what He sees in full.

There are no magical keys to decipher the visual encryption of a work of art.   There is only the call to walk by faith, asking God to take our hand and guide our feet as we walk this visual journey together. I will pray for you as you take your next steps.

—

Exercise Three:
Visual Lectio Divina

This exercise is designed to help you experience what you read in the previous section. The idea of prayer of the hand is simple enough if you consider how visual art is one of the languages of non-verbal prayer. God invites us to have a visual conversation with Him through inspiration, and we as artists answer this invitation by speaking back to God with the vocabulary of visual art. This is the beginning of a non-verbal dialogue with God.

To experience this idea, take your Bible and select a Psalm that speaks to your heart. Look for a word, a phrase, and idea, an image that captures your attention. Consider why these words get your attention, or what God would want you to think about as a result of reading these words. You could similarly listen to someone read the psalm aloud to think about these same things. Some people find it helpful to read or listen to multiple translations or paraphrases of the psalm they select to better understand the nuances of the words.

After finding your inspirational words, take out an index card or a small piece of paper and draw, paint, or scribble a response to these words. Your response is your own, and is not intended to be a polished work of art you will frame later. It is about spending time with God, through drawing, and can only be evaluated based on how truly aware of being in God's presence you were. Once you have finished, reflect on this art privately, or discuss your experience with a small group.

Many people are surprised doing this exercise, as they find that it is easier than they thought it would be. Many people find that they have anxiety about making art, and that only after immersing themselves in the experience for a while are they able to put these concerns aside and be fully present to the activity. Some people may find that this is a truly good surprise, and may want to repeat this exercise at home as a way to use this kind of non-verbal prayer language with God on a regular basis.

―

part four –
the prayer of
the moment

YOU HEAR MY CRY

focus

But when you pray, go into
your room, close the door and
pray to your Father, who is
unseen. Then your Father,
who sees what is done in
secret, will reward you.

Matthew 6:6

I am not a strong intellectual, though I would
hardly say that I am an ignorant man. I have
been writing to you about how to look at art and
understand it, particularly from a Christian
perspective. What I have been sharing with you is
my personal perspective as one person, my
perspective as an artist. I have read some books,
some even by Christians, about how a person
comes to look at and understand art. I would
encourage you to read some of these books as
well. However, my perspective is not so much
informed by reading as by seeing and painting.
Many books written by thinkers about art begin

with examining a piece of finished art, and develop their ideas about the purpose and use of art from that point forward. These writers find value in reflecting on a piece of art that they see before them, but this is not the only value that art can have. For myself, the creation of a painting has value even before the piece is finished. I find that the very act of painting is itself valuable, even when what I make never makes it to a finished state. I refer to this idea as the "prayer of the moment", as each of these creative times are moments spent making art –my form of prayer · in the presence of God. For this reason, I find these moments valuable. The reason is that for me as an artist, what makes the act of painting valuable is not the finished product but the process of creation, which is precious. Let me be clear. When I am talking about the process of creation, I am talking about more than the transfer of paint to canvas; I am talking about the deeper process in the mind of the artist. This is the focus I have while making art which I consider having the deepest value. It is this focus, which I believe deepens with longer and longer times spent marinating in the presence of our creator God. This is the God who gives me inspiration, the ability to imagine, and the ability to express these ideas in visual form. Only my God and my mind know the transactions that take place emotionally, visually and spiritually during the times I create. When I focus on these three things, my art takes on a different kind of value and meaning. These are holy times spent near the heart of God.

What I want to share with you now is a glimpse into this inner way of knowing art. I am aware that there are theoreticians that may deeply disagree with some of the things I will tell you, some of whom have ideas quite different from my own. I respect them and their ideas, because they take art and art-making seriously enough to think about it. At the same time, I want to focus on telling you my own perspective, as one artist, who is speaking only for myself. I find that very few artists read the theoreticians, and I am not sure why that is. I myself do not consider myself anti-intellectual, though when given a choice between reading about art and making it, I more often than not will head to my easel than my bookcase (though curiously my art studio is packed with art books which are shelved along an entire wall). But for the moment, I want to tell you a few thoughts I have had over the years about art as prayer.

I have been asked what I mean when I use the words "visual prayer" to describe my art. In fact, some people are greatly perplexed by this term, questioning how some of my paintings could be prayerful. For them, these images are a far cry from their own visual conceptions of prayerfulness. That is fine, as I too have these biases towards some art that I myself find more prayerful. But what I am going to focus on again is not the finished art product as being intrinsically "prayerful" or not, I want to focus on

———

the thoughts of the artist during the process of creation as determining the "prayerful" quality of the art.

When I look at my own work, some of the paintings that I have made I would have to honestly say are not "prayerful". When I focus primarily on technique, composition, or some other portion of the execution of a piece of art, I find that my mental energies are focused on the details of creating and no longer free to encounter God. Let me give you an example.

I recently have been working with a narrower canvas than I have previously worked with. Though it is only a few inches shorter across the bottom, this change in scale literally cramped my compositions. I did not realize how my mind has grown accustomed to composing within a 3x4 space, and the shift to a 3x5 space really seemed to bother me. I typically start my acrylic paintings by making a light sketch in chalk on the surface of my canvas before starting, a technique which I have become dependant on as a "rough draft" and practice session for my painting. I was so frustrated · drawing, then wiping the chalk away, mixing paint and chalk, then painting out the paint, scraping it down, walking away... I was having such trouble composing. I must have created three or four complete sketches, becoming dissatisfied with one element or another in each of them. I began to despair that I was only repeating my previous work, that I had run out of ideas, and that I no longer had any more thoughts worth painting. My wife stopped in my studio, and we talked. She wisely encouraged me to stop working and wait until I was drawing in church on Sunday for more ideas, as it was obvious that I was unable to focus at that moment.

I was too consumed by the task of composing that I could not step back and allow myself to feel in the presence of God. I was trying to force things into happening. You cannot force yourself on God, you can only meet God by being open to Him, but being equally accepting of the possibility that God may not open your senses to His presence either. When art becomes prayer, I am no longer concerned with the outcome of the work, I am just relishing the moment that I am creating, and am simultaneously aware that I am with God.

This is a difficult concept to put into words, especially as I don't hear many artists talk about this. When at critiques, I often hear artists talk about the technical details of creating, how they struggled with their materials or found difficulty capturing the content of their idea visually. While both of these things are valid concerns, they are roadblocks to praying while making art, as they both take up mental energies. For example, a heavy focus on making things "look real" or illustrating a Biblical scene with historical accuracy, can be anxiety provoking for some

———

people, changing the art making time into a problem-solving exercise rather than a time to engage emotionally and imaginatively with the creator God. Now, some people may find themselves drawn heavily into the presence of God by working in a naturalistic manner or along Biblical-historical lines. I am not so much talking about the choice of subject matter as the emotional arousal level caused by the execution of the work. To better understand how art making can be prayerful, artists who become frustrated with their skills in naturalistic rendering may want to consider non-objective, abstract, or patterned subject matter as a means to create something visual in a prayerful way. The point is, art can be prayer when we allow God to have an opportunity to move our hands, our imaginations, or perceive the little ways He reveals Himself while our eyes are fixed on the art in front of us.

I want to write to you more about this in the coming letters, but for now want you to savor and reflect on the ways that God wants you to focus on Him in whatever you find yourself doing today.

—

PSALM 26

ingredients of prayer

May these words of my mouth
and this meditation of my heart
be pleasing in your sight.
LORD. my Rock and my
Redeemer.

Psalm 19:14

I want to share with you now some of the things
that I consider "prayerful practices" which some
artists have when working and conceiving a piece
of art. I am not sure that I can speak for all
artists here, but I can speak for myself and make
some generalizations based on the artists I know
well.

As I pointed out before, artists can focus on many
things when they work, some of which they are
aware of, and some of which they may never
come to recognize. I think that much is clear.
However, when the act of creating takes on a
prayerful quality, the artist transitions out of a
state of intentionality about the work, and moves

into a state of expression. I like to think of it as moving from the head to the heart. We can't help but be consumed by the activity of making to the point that the very creative act becomes something that we no longer need to think about. It is like walking. I have been watching as my youngest daughter is beginning to walk now. Each time she takes a step, it is deliberate. She has her head down, watching her feet move, sometimes placing each footstep down with more force than needed so that it reverberates like a drum on the wooden floor of our home. At times she even appears fearful, as if the thought of falling the small distance to the floor would crush her tender hopes for mobility. She needs to focus on the task of walking. My older daughter has been walking for two years, and at this point no longer looks at her feet, she looks ahead, often hurtling her body through space, jumping off of furniture, and dancing in the middle of the living room floor. For her, the act of stepping is no longer something that she needs to be mindful of. For her, movement itself is a joy. This is so much like art making. When art becomes prayer, our working time moves from walking to dancing.

When we begin to dance with our art materials, what gets expressed often comes out of the depths of the heart. I find for myself that many of the artists that I greatly admire who seem to have a prayerful quality to their art also possess this kind of attitude about their work. Their art becomes a record of their inner journey, and perhaps takes less concern for rendering naturalistically as much as capturing a sense of mood. This is what impacts me also as a viewer, though right now I do not want to digress into talking to you about how we as viewers can pray with art. Suffice it to say here (and then I will get back to the topic) that if the artist prays while making the art, others who see the art-product will likely also sense this as well, at least those with eyes to see it. Artists who pray seem to want to deal with the *emotional* qualities of their lives, often dealing with dreamlike imagery, psychological issues, or things from their present reality or their past. Even when an artist's work does not have identifiable subject matter, this work seems to use the visual architecture of design to communicate a sense or a spirit that would be difficult to express any other way. Art captures for a moment the kind of expression that a gesture in dance similarly conveys. This kind of prayerful art is the aroma, which blossoms from the perfume of the heart.

This kind of art seems to also capture a sense of mystery, poetically pairing the recognizable with the unidentifiable, altering objects aesthetically, or conveying a sense of playfulness or whimsy. There is something "non-literal" about this kind of art. Even now, I am feeling that desire to show you examples as these kinds of things are so difficult to express in words. Can you imagine what I am talking about here? By visually speaking the language of the heart, the artist begins to fashion work that prays to God during that holy moment of creation.

Let me push this idea further, if I may. Imagine doing a commissioned painting for someone who, instead of wanting to hire you to create an image that they have in their head, wants you to create a work of art about a struggle that they are having in their life, knowing full well that the time it takes to create the peace is time spent in a sort of aesthetic intercessory prayer on their behalf. I would love to pray like that for people. Imagine a church whose walls were adorned with these kinds of visual prayers for their people. What kind of visual impact would this kind of art have on those who entered the doors? I love to think about such things. These kinds of daydreams about how art could impact the church are like the kiss of rain that baptizes soil pregnant with seed.

My friend, I pray that what I am writing makes sense to you. I hope you begin to see what I am talking about, how I feel when I make art in the presence of God, art that directly impacts my relationship with God at that moment... art that comes through me and may speak to me as well. Art making is probably the way that God gets my attention best. I believe this art may come from my imagination, but it is not my own. It belongs to God. It is my deepest desire that all people find this kind of creative connection with God.

———

My friend, I hope you also find ways to have this kind of intimate relationship as well.

———

to pray with art

For since the creation of the
world God's invisible
qualities–his eternal power
and divine nature–have
been clearly seen, being
understood from what has
been made, so that people
are without excuse.

Romans 1:20

I want to tell you (now that you understand how
an artist prays while making art in the presence
of God) how each of us can learn to view art in the
presence of God. You see, we are always in God's
presence. He surrounds us, though so often we
are unaware of this. So whatever we do, we are
doing it while simultaneously being totally
encircled by God. We walk, do the dishes, get
dressed, go to work, take care of others,
socialize... all in the presence of God. We even
make and view art in the presence of God. And

when we take a moment to reflect on God while viewing a work of art, we begin to pray visually.

St. Augustine, the great African theologian, wrote that the whole world is composed of "signs" pointing towards God. I propose that works of art can be one of those signs which capture and reflect some sense of God's presence, or that in some way cause us to reflect prayerfully on a situation.

Though my bias is that "Christian art" can only be created by Christians, I believe that any created thing (made by believing hands or not) can be viewed by Christians in a prayerful manner. In other words, any thing, when used by God, can be a visual call to prayer.

My friend, you may be asking what a "prayerful" way to view art is. Let me explain. When we pray with words, our intention should be to reflect for a moment on God's relationship with us, speaking to Him as a person, aware that He hears us and wants to relate to us. When we pray with our eyes, a similar thing occurs.

The act of looking, particularly at art, is a reflective activity. Notice that art galleries and museums typically are quiet environments, places intentionally created to promote this kind of "extended looking". It is the artist's goal to call you to ponder the visual poem before your eyes, thinking for a moment about its mood, it's meaning, or its maker. Quite possibly, when praying visually, God may want you to think about these very things as well. This can be a way to meditate on your relationship with God, your relationship with others, or something God draws you to contemplate.

I can think of many examples from my own life when I have viewed art prayerfully. Often, while looking at paintings, I am struck by a sense of wonder and awe, and begin thanking God in the quietness of my heart that He allowed a glimpse of His goodness to show through the rendering of the image before me. I may be stunned by the intricate or spontaneous brushwork, the choice of colors, or the power of the composition. In other cases, my heart may cry out at images that I find disturbing, particularly with depictions of a lewdly sexual nature or graphic violence. I find myself needing to work through these difficult emotions to get to the point that I can pray for the person who created these images. Sometimes the artist has already died, or I am not aware of the origins of the piece. At these times, I pray for people who feel the kinds of emotions that the artist is portraying. Other works of art strike me neither with awe or repulsion, they just appear banal to me. In these cases, I may be confused about what the meaning is or the spirit in which the piece was conceived. These works remind me that I do not have all the answers and that there are so many things that I have not the eyes to understand yet. I pray at these times that God open my heart to try to understand these expressions, as well as people who express things that I do not identify with. And at other times, I may walk away from an exhibit with a sense that the world I am living in is deeply broken, either concerned with things of no ultimate value or that people are wrestling with pain at a very profound level. This is when my heart feels most open, and I pray for the world. As I write this, I am struck by this most profoundly, that much art created today seems to mock or express sadness. So often, my recent gallery trips leave me with a sense that the creative people living today have such heaviness inside of them. They truly need prayer.

You may have other kinds of responses when you view art, which is to be expected. I am only sharing a few of the typical responses that I have to works of art, responses that I am learning to perceive as cues to prayer. In the stillness of the gallery space, I believe that if we are perceptive, we are able to hear the still, small whispering voice of God among the pieces.

I hope you are beginning to have a sense of this as well.

—

Gbemi Jesu

finding God in the gallery

I do not concern myself with
great matters
or things too wonderful for me.
But I have calmed myself
and quieted my ambitions...
... put your hope in the
LORD
both now and forevermore.

Psalm 131: 1b-2a; 3

In my last letter, I talked about hearing the quiet voice of the Holy Spirit whispering in your ear while viewing art. That is one way to imagine God's presence while in a gallery. But I want you to join with me for a moment and imagine it being another way.

Many people talk about art that portrays overt, religious subject matter as being a "window" through which people pray to God. I do not want to argue with this viewpoint exactly, but I do want to challenge it, especially as many contemporary works of art deal with the surface of the work as an end in itself. No longer is naturalistic depiction and perspective drawing the only means by which to think of art, particularly as these techniques treat the surface of the work as if it were a window, with the subject of the work receding beyond the frame. No. In this current day and age, a work of art may be entirely about the treatment of the surface of a painting. Furthermore, from a theological viewpoint, I believe that more and more Christians are aware that God is surrounding us at all times, and that we are not reaching out to this far distant God though windows, or intercessors, or other means. Instead, we need only to open our hand as He already within reach and so desires to clasp our hand and walk with us. God is always here with us, and He may be using art as one of many ways to remind us of this fact, refocusing our spiritual eyesight to perceive the signs of His presence that are around us all the time.

So erase from your imagination for the moment the idea that God is somehow beyond you, accessible through the window of a piece of art, or floating up in space somewhere above the clouds. Imagine instead that the world as you know it is submerged in God, like a fish is surrounded by the water of the ocean. In this way of thinking, God is immediately near you, beside you, in front of you, behind you... everywhere. Looking at a piece of art, you are looking literally through God while He is simultaneously beside you. The process of looking at the art does not somehow bring you close to God, because He is already close to you, but it may remind you of God. I imagine that fish rarely are aware of the fact that they are swimming in water either until they are pulled out of it for a minute, gasping because they no longer feel the pressure of it against their bodies. This is like our God · the God who walks with us, looks with us, and imagines with us.

However, the dirt of distraction so often clouds our vision that we spend too much time focusing on these tiny particles and loose sight of God. We need to teach ourselves to "look past" the things that would normally capture our attention in order to maintain our focus. I imagine a similar scenario is driving a car through a nighttime blizzard. The snow, falling all about the car, appears to be rushing the headlights as the car flies down the winter road, the black of the sky an oppressive contrast to the blinding snow. But if you are driving, you cannot focus on looking at the swooping flakes as you would quickly become disoriented and slide off the road. Instead, you must train your eye to look past the flakes, tracking the edge of the road so that you can keep your vehicle on the street. In many ways, works of art function as the "edge of the road" in this manner, objects on which we can focus our vision so that we can remember what is important. These art objects that take on this spiritual role can be reminders of God, objects that have no special value in themselves, but whose presence does remind us of the God who created everything.

So this is another way of thinking of how to see God in a gallery.

Last evening, I was walking through the narthex of my own church with a group from our congregation who were brainstorming ways to turn this very stark, utilitarian room into a functional, aesthetic space that could be used to draw people into the presence of God through art displays. It was a wonderful moment of excited energy, ideas, and dreams of taking something plain and making it beautiful. We discussed changes in the lighting, the walls, and looked at ways to re-structure the space so that the room would be a place where people may want to linger to meet God with their eyes, as opposed to a place that people rushed through mindlessly. But what I hoped most of all is that this is a place where people come to hear God, but find themselves seeing God as well, even if it was not what they expected to do. Who knows, maybe some of those who pass through this space will come to sense the presence of God as powerfully

in these outer courts as in the inner court of the
sanctuary itself.

———

Joy

benediction

But you have an anointing
from the Holy One,
and all of you know the truth.

I John 2:20

I want to share one more thing with you in
closing. For the past decade, a group of artists,
poets, writers, music composers, and dancers
who attend my church have met regularly to
share and pray. This creative community has
been invaluable to all of us as a place where we
find a sense of belonging. At each of our
gatherings, before we leave, we have a way that
we bless each other.

It often is quiet in the room. Our meetings often
are times when we laugh, sometimes cry, and are
almost always thoughtful. But when we end, it is
quiet. We have just had a verbal prayer for each
other, or sometimes decide to sit silently in the
presence of God. Upon opening our eyes, we
open our palms, holding them open to each

———

other. I begin, taking a small cup of water and wetting my finger. I turn to the person sitting next to me, and make the sign of the cross on each of their hands with the water. While looking into their eyes, I say, "May God bless you, as you go and create." Then, the cup is passed, and each person blesses the person next to him or her, until everyone has been blessed by someone. The room is filled with quiet smiles, open hands, and a palpable sense of the presence of God.

So, to close, I want to bless you too.

May God bless *you*, as you go and create.

Amen.

Exercise Four: Gallery Prayer

In this final exercise, take some time to spend with God walking in a gallery, noticing the art there with a heart open to having God get your attention there. If you do not have access to a gallery, consider doing this exercise with a piece of art you find meaningful in your home, or in another public place where art is displayed. Do this exercise as you did the noticing prayer in exercise two, only this time take notice of the artwork, taking time to soak in the presence of one or two pieces.

Record your prayer time verbally, visually, or any other way you see fit.

Reflect on your experience, and consider talking about this with a small group. For a deeper discuss of this topic, read the material in Appendixes 1 and 2 before you go to prepare your heart to be with God in this space.

appendix 1 – questions for discussion

These questions are intended to be "conversation starters" and not a series of questions intended to be strictly followed. Feel free to add your own questions, observations, or remarks when leading a group using this book. The art of the discussion is up to you. These questions were initially designed for discussion with visual artists or mixed groups of "creative types", though slight modifications could be easily made for groups of general church members. Of course, the general questions "What did this make you think about?" or "Does anyone have a reflection on this?" are always good discussion starters for any group. You may want to challenge group members to think of scripture references to support their viewpoints.

Introduction

Think of a person who you know who does not understand your art? What would be one thing that you would want to share with this person about your creative endeavors? What do you think people commonly misunderstand about you or your work? What do people seem to understand well? How do you feel about sharing your work because of these responses?

———

Part One – Foundational Ideas

On Words

How have creative people in your church been employed? What kinds of expression are not often or ever used? What would happen if they were? What are the particular strengths and weaknesses of your particular church or denomination (be as specific as you can)? How could the creative arts be used to build on the strengths of your particular church body?

Intimacy With God

How do you find intimacy with God? Do you have particular practices that you employ, or do you experience God in many ways? What places are you likely to encounter God in your home or daily routine?

Pray Without Speaking

This letter begins to explore the idea that not all prayers need to be ones that are spoken. Take the idea of "silent prayer." How did you come to understand what "silent prayer" was? Is it verbal or non-verbal? Contrast this idea with the notion of sacrifices in the Old Testament. How are burnt offerings and silent (verbal) prayers similar? What do you think a silent prayer that did not use words would be like? How does the idea of "centering prayer" fit between spoken and silent prayer? Have you ever prayed like this? What was the result?

Seeing God

Through most of the history of the church, controversy has existed about the use of visual images in the church, particularly in worship. Artists have felt the effects of these tensions. This letter addresses the idea that there is a visual element to Christianity and that faith itself has a visual nature to it. How do you feel about using your artistic gifts in your church? Where would you use them if you do not presently do so? How do you think your church's teachings affect the way you think of the role of the visual arts in worship? How do these teachings affect your feelings about the use of art in general?

Balanced Meals

Read Deuteronomy 6:4-7 and Matthew 22:36-38. Jesus quotes the Old Testament law in Matthew. Notice that the words for "heart" and "soul" are translated in English using the same word, but that the word for "strength" also can be understood as "mind." What do you think this could mean? Many churches emphasize a more action-oriented or cognitively oriented understanding of what it means to be a "good" Christian. How do you struggle to love God with both your strength and mind? Where do you need to supplement your spiritual diet? Where might you need to cut back? Is there another person who could guide or mentor you in learning to balance your spiritual diet?

Learning to Remember

Do you know someone who shows their giftedness in a way that was not nurtured in school? Are you someone like this? What ideas do you hold about who is smart and who is not? What kinds of people do you know who you respect that may have strong gifts in one of the less-often-recognized intelligences?

Many artists who don't like talking about their work hold to the idea that their art "speaks for itself." Many churches do not incorporate visual elements as a regular part of worship. How might the ideas in the Learning Pyramid challenge these positions? How could you be challenged to grow by these ideas?

Art as Prayer

If God were to open you up right now, what would He find inside?

Part Two – The Prayer of the Eye

Aesthetic Prayer

Read 1 Corinthians 12:12-27. After reading this, what additional spin does the concept "prayer of the eye" have? If the church were all made of one body part, what do you think it would look like (besides very creepy)? Do you think that any of the body parts listed in the passage have been ignored or over-used by the body?

Look at the last paragraph of the text. If God were writing a love letter to you right now, what would He be saying to you? Where do you "soak in" the messages?

Assumptive Awareness

The concept of God's omnipotence is cited in this letter. When are you most aware of God? What are the grains of sand in your life where you have had private encounters with God? What kinds of things blind you from seeing God? As an artist, do you ever think of making art "in the presence of God?" Why or why not?

Be Still and Know

What environment(s) do you find sacred or holy? What makes these places feel this way? When was the last time you spent more than 10 minutes focused on God? What do you think God would reveal to you if you "stilled and quieted your soul"? How could being still and quiet in this manner affect your art making?

Anticipative Observing

When are you most aware of God's omnipotent presence? What fosters this kind of awareness in you? Where do you go to get ideas? Do you feel aware of God when you are inspired? What kinds of experiences get your attention to remind you of God? How frequent are these experiences? What do you think would need to happen in your life to have more experiences like this?

Reflective Perceiving

How does what is written in the beginning of this section relate to the idea in the book of James that "faith without works is dead?" What kind of visual "calls to prayer" (e.g. inspirations to create art, notions that you need to meditate or focus on God etc.) have you experienced lately? How has the way that God created you to be affected the way you pray and the things you think of to pray/create about?

Meditative Recording

What are some things that you appreciate (or find awe-inspiring) but do not fully understand? What artistic things do you feel you understand, at least somewhat? Have you ever thought about art making as a way to pray? Why or why not? What does your art say about your relationship to God? Are there some of these artistic prayers that cause you to pause? What would the reasons be for this? If you were to make a card to send to God right now, what would the card look like? If there were words inside, what would they say?

Part Three – The Prayer of the Hand

Artistic Prayer

How can interacting with materials be a form of prayer? Can you think of any way that God has spoken through inanimate objects in scripture, or can you imagine or recall a time that God spoke through materials to you? If you are working on a piece of art right now, what technical problems or conceptual issues are you experiencing? How could God use these situations to speak to you right now if you took a moment to reflect on them? God knows our thoughts and hearts, though sometimes what is in our heart is not communicated well through our hands. Knowing this, how do you think that others see our work verses the way that God does?

The Aesthetic Chapel

What activities help you to clear your mind of anxiety and concerns so that you can focus on the moment at hand? Looking at combing these activities with the idea of "place", where would you say that you could go to best focus on God? Look up passages in the Bible where people intentionally went somewhere to be with God. How is where they went similar or different from where you go? Do you ever think of where you make art as one of these kinds of places? Do you ever feel that your creative place is "holy ground?"

Alternate Sanctuaries

Describe a time when doing something physical helped you to focus on something else. Imagining your home, where could you go to let your mind wander? If you cannot let your mind wander, or come up with a list of reasons why you cannot get this kind of focus, identify what is taking up your mental energy. Could this energy be allocated another way, or is there a way that you could re-direct it? Imagine when you were a new Christian or a young child and first became aware of God. Where were you when this experience happened?

The Rhythm of Creation

Honestly look at your creative pattern (maybe even take out a blank calendar page and identify the days and times you have devoted to creating). How would you describe your present creative pattern? How do you personally feel about structured living (e.g. is this something you enjoy, strive for, avoid, resent etc.)? Evaluate how structured your life is in general, looking at your daily schedule, financial budged, eating habits, and calendar. Do you find that you structure your own life, that others structure your life for you, or that you have an unstructured life? What are the positive and negative aspects of your lifestyle choices? How do you think God wants you to use your time?

The Artist's Prayer

Do you find yourself to have time for mystery, wonder and reflection? In terms of roles, do you think that visual art making can work as a form of prayer, or do you think it should play a different role in a person's life? Art is one of those things in life that takes time to understand. Are there other things in your life that have taken time to understand (as opposed to things that you feel you understand almost immediately)? If God could open your eyes to see the way He sees, how do you think your impressions of people would change? How could it affect the way you see art?

Part Four – The Prayer of the Moment

Focus

What visual images enter your mind when you think of prayer? What works of art do you find reminiscent of prayer? How do these images inform you when you think of making your own "prayerful art?" Do you think that a viewer can detect art made in the spirit of prayer afterwards? When you pray with words, do you personally focus on how you want the outcome of the prayer to be, or are you focused on "being with God in the moment?" What kind of things can aid you in being more focused on the "being with God" moment?

Ingredients of Prayer

Think of times when prayer seemed for you to move from walking to dancing. Have you ever felt like this? Do you know any artists that work in a prayerful way, or whose

—

work has a quality that brings you close to God? What elements of the artist's person (or of their work) appear prayerful to you? What colors, subject matter, or media speak prayerfully to you? Could this be your artistic prayer language?

To Pray With Art

After reading this section, what would be some ways that you could pray for artists in general? Do you ever think of art as a visual "call to prayer"? If you do not personally pray "with" art, what things do get your attention to remind you to pray? Knowing that all artists are expressing ideas, how could you better pray for individual artists after seeing their work?

Finding God in the Gallery

Take a moment to draw two pictures – one of an idea of God that you used to believe, but that is incorrect. The second picture should represent an image of God that you do find more correct now. Share these pictures and discuss them. This section contrasts a distant God with a God of immediacy. Do you find this to be true for you? What kinds of distractions recently prevented you from experiencing God? If you have overcome them, talk about how this was achieved. If you are still struggling, do you know how to re-focus?

Benediction

How are you dismissed from your church service? What do you do with your posture, your eyes, and your hands? If you have a traditional dismissal, what words typically are spoken? How do these patterns shape you? What would it feel like to have your hands anointed? When you think of what God would want to say to you often, what do you think God would want you to hear?

appendix 2 –
art as prayer: a way of prayer

As an artist and a Christian, I find it fascinating to hear people talk about their prayer life. Many people find deep meaning in following conventional methods of prayer, and some even find strength in reading or speaking written prayers. Yet, for me, I find it interesting to hear the stories and to listen to people describe their methods which are less conventional means to know God. For myself, I find that I grow closest to God through the process of making art, noting that each step along the way is a means of prayer, a way of becoming more intimate with God. Here are some of the exercises that I have found helpful to me.

The prayer of the eye

This is often where ideas begin, the notion that I as an artist "see" something (whether real or in my imagination) that give me an artistic idea. I believe that God is continuously surrounding us, wanting us to be more aware of His constant presence. These moments when I "see" something, which gives me an idea, are a means that I now recognize as God "getting my attention." This kind of "holy noticing" is what I believe is the prayer of the eye.

So to pray the prayer of the eye is to focus on observing, noticing, and being aware of both God and the world around us. When we are able to balance both of these things, we become more in tune with

The prayer of the hand

If God speaks visually to us, I find it natural as an artist to reply back to God in a similar manner. My hands are the lips with which I speak my prayer back to God through the language of the visual. In this way I imagine that God and I commune and communicate back and forth as I visually flesh-out my idea first as a sketch, then as I respond in the moment to the paint on my canvas as I work the image there. This back-and-forth visual communication is a way that I spend long stretches of quiet time in the presence of God, completing the circle of visual communication.

The prayer of the moment

Each painting captures a moment in time, a moment that has a definite beginning and which ends when the painting is complete. The ideas, emotions, struggles, and joys of creating are permanently recorded in the surface of the paint, a visual utterance of my prayers frozen in time. At this point, the actual painting itself moves from an process to an object, which can in turn be responded to when used to begin a prayer of the eye. Each person who views a piece of art and reflects on it (while in an awareness of God's presence) is similarly praying a "prayer of the eye", the kind of artistic prayer that begins the prayer cycle yet again.

appendix 3 – the seven learning/worship styles

If you are reading this, you may have taken the Multiple Intelligences quiz from http://www.businessballs.com/freepdfmaterials/free_multiple_intelligences_test_manual_version.pdf mentioned in Exercise 1. The results of this questionnaire indicate likely styles or pathways you use to understand the world and relate to God. There are no superior or inferior styles, though every culture may emphasize or value certain styles more than others. However, this is not how God views us.

Read about your styles below, and imagine how knowing about your style can help you understand and relate to God even more. At the end of each section, there are some suggested starting points for understanding visual art using this style. These are suggestions, not rules, since having a sense of wonder is the most powerful tool in learning to understand visual art.

Linguistic: People who learn and worship in the linguistic style are able to take and process information better with words and language than some other ways of getting information. They would prefer to understand ideas through written and spoken words, and interpret ideas through language. These people are also curious about the meanings of words, as well as more subtle differences in meaning based on word choice and the tone people use when speaking words. People with this style often find themselves in careers that similarly put a high emphasis on written and spoken words. In Protestant worship in particular, the emphasis on worship being about the word of God has made a unique and necessary role for the use of this style in worship. People with this style may sometimes have difficulty understanding how people with non-verbal styles can process ideas on a level equal to theirs, if they do not also know how to learn and worship in a non-verbal style as well. These difficulties may be tempered if the Linguistic person learns to use their verbal strengths to patiently ask questions of those with other styles, thereby learning more about these other styles through their preferred verbal style. In terms of understanding visual art, people with the linguistic style may find talking or writing to be ways they understand visual art best. For example, thinking of questions to ask about artists or artwork may be helpful starting points to understanding what some visual art means. Also, becoming familiar with the language artists use to critique their work may give further tools for unpacking artwork, as would reading about art history.

Logical-Mathematical: People who learn and worship in a logical-mathematical style process information best through logical thinking. This means that numbers, logical ideas, and measurable outcomes are highly valued and needed for people with a logical-mathematical style to take ideas to heart. People with this style tend to gravitate towards jobs and tasks that take analytical thinking, organization, or troubleshooting. Those with a leaning towards processing ideas using numbers often find employment in the theoretical or applied sciences, or other careers that rely heavily on numbers or analyzing data. However, a smaller number who lean more towards processing ideas with words may find a way to use their style to structure and organize systems of thought, and may find a lifelong interest in fields such as philosophy or theology. People with this style may worship well when the ideas in worship are expressed logically and with consistency. If not tempered by strong Interpersonal or Intrapersonal strengths, people with this style may find inconsistencies in policies and other people's behavior to be extremely frustrating. People with this gift who have strong Interpersonal gifts may find themselves to be quite effective in administrative leadership roles. In terms of understanding visual art, people with a mathematical/logical style may find insight into art through learning about compositional analysis, and may find this kind of structural approach to looking at art a helpful place to begin. Reading the work of the great art critic Clement Greenberg may provide an additional reference point for this approach.

Musical: People who learn and worship in a musical style have a deep awareness, appreciation, and use for music in their lives. They deeply sense how the verbal and non-verbal aspects of music can equally express mood and emotion, often joining the two in song. People with this style will often process and understand ideas when they find them expressed artistically in song or non-verbal music. While few find careers in this area, many people with a musical style find a plethora of non-career uses for using their gifts. Musicians and singers have had a long history of being used in worship, and often find these gifts to be easily used in multiple settings in the church. This historic dominance in worship may lead those with these giftings to have difficulty imagining how non-performance-based gifts can be used in worship, unless they personally are able to use a non-verbal style to worship as well. When people with a musical style do not similarly possess equally strong linguistic or logical-mathematical styles, there may be periodic times of conflict with other church leaders over the lyrics of songs used in worship. When learning to appreciate visual art, notice the compositional strategies that music and visual art have in common. While both music and visual art utilize the non-verbal aspects of expression, the vocabulary of visual art uses line, color, texture, shape etc. in place of tone, melody, dynamics, and tempo. Learning about artists whose work was a visual response to music or sound may prove to be inspiring.

Bodily-Kinesthetic: People with a bodily-kinesthetic style learn best through activity, using their bodies to process and understand information. People with this style use their gifts in many fields, often pairing this style with an additional style to find success making or repairing things, expressing themselves with their bodies, or engaging in physical sports and play. In worship, people with this style will more than any other style want to respond physically with moment or posture to process the ideas presented in a service. In fact, for people with this style, it is movement itself that imbues ideas with power, literally wanting to be "moved" by what they experience. These worshipers will retain and process ideas through movement, dance, clapping, and symbolic or ritual interaction. Historically, people with this learning and worship style have been misperceived as being unconcerned with the spiritual aspects of worship and life, and have been viewed with suspicion in worship in some circles. This history may need to be addressed by church leadership if this history has had a strong role in a congregation before people with this style may want to use their style in worship. When learning to understand visual art, people with a bodily-kinesthetic style may find parallels between the implied movement of static visual art and the actual movement through space of the human form. Figurative and gestural artwork may be particularly inspiring. You may find inspiration for lighting and costume ideas from viewing visual art as well as performance or installation pieces.

Visual-Spatial: People with a visual-spatial style learn through the visual arts. For this type of person, ideas and concepts that can be expressed through objects, artwork, or relationships between images are easily digested. People who use this style often find they are able to use it in fields requiring attention to visual things, such as graphic design, photography, studio art, engineering, beauty salons, architecture and town planning. People with the visual-spatial style who do not also possess Linguistic or Interpersonal styles may find it difficult or intimidating to explain their style to others, and may actually take measures to avoid doing so (often leading to an increased sense of being misunderstood and isolated). However, those with the Visual-Spatial style who also have a strong Intrapersonal style will often find solace in developing a uniquely personal mode of expression that will continue to deepen over time, which may be very useful to share with others to enrich them. In worship, those with a visual-spatial style may find that they need to draw or doodle to engage with very verbal or logical portions of a worship service. They may also tend to have a rich visual experience when praying, that may have prophetic overtones that need to be honed with a mentor. They will be drawn to anything visual in the worship space, and will particularly feel ministered to by the active employment of visual media in all aspects of worship, particularly if it is paired with verbal gifts. Understanding visual art will come naturally for people with this style, though they too may not automatically understand every piece of art. However, since visual creations are the heart-language of this style of understanding the world and connecting to God, comprehending other artists and artworks will be more intuitive for people with this style than any other style.

Interpersonal: Both Interpersonal and Intrapersonal styles are indicator styles, meaning that they indicate how deeply an individual uses their emotional intelligence outward towards relating to others (Interpersonal) or inwardly towards understanding their own self (Intrapersonal). In many ways the Interpersonal style can be understood as the classic extrovert – a person who draws energy and inspiration from relating to others. In this case, the Interpersonal style indicates an ability to perceive other people's feelings, particularly in interpersonal relationships of any kind. These people may find that they can use their style effectively as therapists and healers, teachers, politicians, coaches, or even in sales and marketing. In worship, people who exhibit this style will find that they process the ideas presented in a service through interactions with others, through discussion, and through group activities. People with this style may find themselves drawn to ministries that rely in hospitality in its various forms. When

———

learning about artists and artwork, having conversations with artists or talking about art with a group of people may be important in processing the possible meanings of artworks. Since many visual artists work in solitude, people with this style may need to approach artists to discuss their work in more intimate settings. These relationships, while needing work, will likely prove rewarding.

Intrapersonal: People with the Intrapersonal style are highly attuned to their inner life. These individuals draw inspiration and energy from ideas and personal reflection, having great strengths in their own self-awareness. This does not mean that people with an Intrapersonal style dislike people, but rather that they are able to draw on their inner resources and find pleasure, rather than discomfort, when they have time alone. People with an intrapersonal style may express the content of their inner journey through any number of forms or styles (such as linguistic, musical, bodily-kinesthetic, or visual-spatial). In worship, people with an Intrapersonal style will want to have times to reflect – often without distraction from words or familiar tunes of songs that may draw their attention away from their inner thoughts. People with an intrapersonal style may find it easy to understand artwork when given time to ponder the meaning of a single piece of art. Since much visual art is intended to be an object of reflection, the person with the intrapersonal style is an ideal candidate to understand and think about a work of art. It may also be interesting for people to process their thoughts about a work of art in a journal or sketchbook to aid their understanding.

About the Author

Eric Nykamp lives in Grand Rapids, Michigan with his wife Yee Lam and their three young children. He attends Madison Square Church where he plays the piano, Hammond organ and djembe drums for a black gospel worship team. In 2001, he began leading a group called "Creative Community", a fellowship of "creative folks" from his congregation. He was the president of GR-CIVA, the Grand Rapids affiliate of CIVA (Christians in the Visual Arts) from 2005-2011. In addition to creating his own art, he helps others discover their inner rhythmic expression as a drum circle facilitator.

For more information about Eric, or to see more of his artwork, visit his websites www.ericnykamp.com and www.ucircles.org

Milton Keynes UK
Ingram Content Group UK Ltd.
UKHW021330310724
1104UKWH00060B/1155